Mike Monteiro

DESIGN IS A JOB

Publisher: Jeffrey Zeldman
Designer: Jason Santa Maria
Editor: Mandy Brown
Copyeditor: Krista Stevens
Compositor: Rob Weychert
Editorial Assistant: Sally Whiting
Production Assistant: Nellie McKesson

ISBN 978-1-937557-04-1

A Book Apart
New York, New York
http://abookapart.com

10 9 8 7 6 5 4 3 2 1

 **A BOOK APART**

Dear Reader—

I once had a client walk me through every corner of his factory. He showed me how each machine tool worked, explained his shipping and inventory systems, fed me in his lunch room, and introduced me to each of his employees. At the end of the tour, he told me, "If your design fails, all these people lose their jobs."

Design is a profession of persuasion. All your talent and experience mean nothing if you can't sell your work to that most anxious of end users, your client. Before you persuade the public to push that button or pinch-zoom that photo spread, you must convince your client to trust you. She must believe in you as a professional who will do your job right, or *all those people lose their jobs*.

Where *HTML5 for Web Designers* and *CSS3 for Web Designers* offered the tools to create modern websites, *Design Is a Job* gives you a platform to build a livelihood. Where *The Elements of Content Strategy* and *Designing for Emotion* showed how to engage the reader, *Design Is a Job* explains how to manage a business engagement. And where *Mobile First* and *Responsive Web Design* showed how to navigate your users' changing contexts, *Design Is a Job* charts a course to sustain you through all the changing contexts of your professional life. On this, there's no better guide than Mule Design's acerbic yet radiant Mike Monteiro.

I think you will love this book. I know you will use it in your daily work, and over the long arc of your career.

Yours,
Jeffrey Zeldman

Jeffrey Zeldman
Publisher

Jason Santa Maria
Designer

Mandy Brown
Editor

TABLE OF CONTENTS

1   *Introduction*

5   CHAPTER 1
What Is a Designer?

11   CHAPTER 2
Getting Clients

22   CHAPTER 3
Choosing the Right Clients

31   CHAPTER 4
Charging for Your Work

45   CHAPTER 5
Working with Contracts

57   CHAPTER 6
Sticking to Your Process

66   CHAPTER 7
Presenting Design

75   CHAPTER 8
Managing Feedback

87   CHAPTER 9
Getting Your Money

100   CHAPTER 10
Working with Others

130   *Conclusion*

132   *Resources*

134   *Acknowledgements*

136   *Index*

This book is dedicated to my son Henry.

Sometimes when you can't find what you need it's just because you haven't made it yet. Now it's your *turn.*

FOREWORD

ONLINE AND OFFLINE, Mike Monteiro is known as a straight talker. He is a living bullshit detector and will not suffer fools. I believe this is because he started his career by making logos in thirty minutes for a copy shop in Austin, without prior qualifications. Fear of discovery is terrible, but it keeps you on your toes. I should know: I started out making logos in thirty minutes for a small printshop in Berlin, without prior qualifications as a graphic designer. So Mike and I know bullshit when we see and hear it, having been quite good at it for a while ourselves.

Being a designer is all about attitude. Sure, you have to know your craft, but as we both found out, you can pick most of that up over time if you're prepared to listen, watch, and learn. Without the right attitude, however, you'll always be a vendor to some people, a crazy artist to others.

Clients need to understand that they've hired us to do something they are not good at. And that they need to pay us for our knowledge, skills, experience and, yes: attitude. To be referred to as one of those "creative types" is to be written off as intellectually inferior.

Contrary to popular belief, designers are not artists. We employ artistic methods to visualize thinking and process, but, unlike artists, we work to solve a client's problem, not present our own view of the world. We thrive on constraints, but we hate compromise. If a design project is to be considered successful—and success is the true measure of quality—it must not only add an aesthetic dimension, but solve the problem at hand.

This book will teach you how to be part of a service industry without becoming a servant. My advice, now and always, is learn, learn, learn—starting right here.

—Erik Spiekermann

INTRODUCTION

I LOVE DESIGN.

I love it when something is well-designed. I love the process of getting there. I love the interesting failures along the way. I love that I have the opportunity to earn a living designing things at a place that my partner and I built from the ground up. I love the arguing and the critiques. I love that someone I hired three years ago can now make *my* designs better. And I absolutely love the clients who make this possible.

Which leaves you. I love *you* most of all. And I am tired of seeing you get your ass kicked because no one taught you better. I am tired of you not getting paid. I am tired of you working nights and weekends. I am tired of you doing spec work because someone has convinced you it will look good in your portfolio. I am tired of you sitting by and hoping the work sells itself.

So I wrote you a book. It has a spine and by the time you're done reading *so will you.*

This book is a guide to making a living as a designer. It contains the fundamentals of being a working designer, including working with clients and others, valuing your work, and getting paid. This book will look at ways to communicate and apply these fundamentals to every aspect of your job. The goal is to expand your view of your job as a designer to include not just your talent, but the business and communication aspects as well.

I made it a short book so you can get back to work.

This book does not contain a "system." At the end of this book you will not run out to buy forty-three index cards. You will not get real. You will not add five items to your bucket list. You will not have to adjust your social media strategy, nor will you unlock a secret. You will have more confidence in yourself and a deeper understanding of your craft.

Why listen to me?

I've been running Mule Design, along with my partner Erika Hall, for almost ten years. Before that I worked at startups, in-house marketing departments, and for other studios. I've been a freelancer, a contractor, and possibly the world's worst employee. I totally lied about being qualified for the first "design job" I ever got, making logos in thirty minutes for the desktop publishing department of a local copy shop in Austin, Texas. I spent years freaking out that someone would finally figure out I had no idea what I was doing.

I started my own design studio for a few reasons. First, I was a terrible employee. I was convinced I could run a design studio better than anyone I'd ever worked for, and I wasn't sure why they had such a difficult time doing it. (Turns out the problem they all had in common was me.)

Second, I wanted control over the kind of clients I worked with. It's my belief that as a designer you are responsible for what you put into the world. When you work for someone else you can't always pick and choose what you work on. We very consciously keep Mule small so we never feel we have to take on a job we can't ethically stand behind just to keep the lights on.

Third, I found a good partner. And I wanted to keep working with her.

Along the way we made every possible mistake we could make. We worked for free. We kept working through shifting strategy. We sat back and waited for the phone to ring. We got shafted. We lost bids for stupid reasons. We worked without contracts. I have made every mistake I am telling you not to make in this book. And I guarantee that you'll make mistakes as well. If not the same ones I did, you'll find new and better ones. Because getting good at what you do doesn't come from not making mistakes; it comes from getting up off the floor after you fall down, and then putting up a warning sign so others avoid the pothole you fell into. This book is my warning sign to you.

Because I want you to do better. And work your ass off. And benefit accordingly. Because design is a job.

Why this book for you

Obviously, try as I might to be balanced, I'm coming at all of this from a bias of client services. And web design. It's what I do. But whether you're in client services, or a freelancer, working at a startup, or a big company, you'll learn something from this book. Heck, you don't even have to be a designer to get something out of this. Whether you call yourself a visual designer, a graphic designer, a web designer, an interaction designer, a photographer, a casual blogger, or a modern dance enthusiast, there will be something in this book that will make you better at your craft.

1

WHAT IS A DESIGNER?

"BRING IN THE CREATIVES!"

"BRING IN THE CREATIVES!"

Let me tell you a beautiful story. You may be living it right now, you lucky dog. This story takes place in a beautiful far-away place with a deep blue sky, an ocean of green-screen possibilities, lollipop-trees dripping with inspiration, and the sensuous dance of exotic muses over the techno-thump of an ambient jungle soundtrack. Yum.

In this beautiful world there are no alarm clocks. After all, creativity demands sufficient sleep. You glide into work when you please, hopping and skipping past the insistent ogres that dare to schedule their beastly requirements meetings before 11 a.m. (there's no need to go to them after 11, either), and you slip into your Mirra chair, dismiss a few meeting requests on your 30″ monitor, fire up iChat, and wait for inspiration to show itself.

By then it's time for lunch.

In this beautiful myth you are what is known as a "creative." You are very lucky. Because while others are weighed down by requirements, metrics, testing, and other variations of math and science, you are a child of magic (or magick, if you're a goth). Knowledge of these base matters would only defile your creative process. Your designs come from inside you.

But, of course, a story isn't really interesting until we introduce a little conflict. Shall we try a dragon? And let's say that dragon is now standing at your desk. And he's holding a printout of your comp, imported into PowerPoint and marked up with very specific changes, most of which you don't agree with—all of them decided in a meeting you did not attend.

Magic won't save you from this dragon. It's time to stop being a creative and start becoming a designer. Grab your lunch. We're clocking in.

WHY THIS MYTH IS DESTRUCTIVE

The myth of the magical creative is alive and well, and it's powerful. It's equally perpetuated by designers and those who work with them. And it's destructive, reducing a designer's job to pixel-pusher, prettifier, and someone who *feels* their way to success. A magical creative is expected to succeed based on instinct, rolling the dice every time, rather than on a methodical process that can be repeated time and time again.

Also, it makes you insufferable. Nobody likes a co-worker who operates outside the rules. And this will make it harder for you to work with your team.

It also makes life harder for other designers (like me) to do their jobs. I love my job. And I don't like people who make it harder than necessary. But every time a client tells me to just "blue sky" something, or that they don't want to "stifle my creativity," I have to spend time undoing the myth of the magical creative. (Luckily, I look more like a Teamster than a magical being, but alas, you may have been cursed with attractiveness.)

A designer requires honest feedback and real criticism, and that's not going to happen in a realm where colleagues or clients are worried about crushing the spirit of a magical being. The sparkly fog of affirmation gets in the way.

So what does a designer actually do? Let's find out.

A DESIGNER SOLVES PROBLEMS WITHIN A SET OF CONSTRAINTS

Those constraints often come in the form of available materials (a lack of wood, a small printing press, or bandwidth), the audience for whom the solution is intended (kids, users who aren't very web-savvy, those who speak a variety of languages), and business requirements (style guides, vendor relationships in place, our logo is Satan).

What kind of problems? Well, that's what determines the kind of designer you are. If you're solving the problem of creating a chair that doesn't hurt your ass if you sit in it for eight hours, you're a furniture designer. If you're sixteen and holding an empty toilet paper roll in one hand and a piece of aluminum foil in the other, you're an industrial designer. Since you're holding one of these small brightly-colored books in your hand, let's assume you're some flavor of web designer, as I am. So for the remainder of this book when I pull out examples or go into specifics, they'll be from a web designer's perspective. If you're a different type of designer I'm sure you can still get something out of this, just abstract it up a level and apply it to your particular field.

A DESIGNER UNDERSTANDS GOALS

Whether you are helping to launch a new business from scratch, or making incremental changes to an existing product, or something in between, any design task you undertake must serve a goal. It's your job to find out what those goals are.

That's the first step to designing anything: ask "Why are we doing this?" If the answer isn't clear, or isn't clear to you, or just doesn't exist, you can't design anything. Stop working. Can you help set those goals? If so, do it. (Yes, it is part of your job. Anything that helps you do your job is part of your job.) How? Coming up.

A DESIGNER GATHERS INFORMATION

Who are we designing for? How will they use what we are designing? Do they need it? What backend technologies does the client have at their disposal? What new ones are they open to trying? Who else has tried this and how have they succeeded or failed?

Once you have design goals you need to gather as much information as possible to make sure you are designing a solution that will fulfill those goals. You simply cannot design without researching the landscape. Just like you can't build a house without surveying the land.

A DESIGNER IMPOSES ORDER

Eventually all of this information needs to be used to create something. Ideas and requirements become artifacts and systems. This is the part of the job most other people will recognize as "design" because it is visible and involves pictures. And you can do it while wearing your headphones.

A DESIGNER CREATES NOVEL FORMS

Also fun. Successful design balances convention—familiar forms, terms, and interactions—and novelty—new forms to engage and delight the users, in the hope they will stick around a bit longer and maybe buy their pants here instead of somewhere else. As long as you remember that those new forms must serve the goals of the business. Otherwise, they're just novelty.

A DESIGNER TALKS TO CLIENTS AND STAKEHOLDERS

No matter how good the work is, if you can't sell it you haven't finished the job. I can't stress how important this is. (I go on at length about this in a later chapter.) I've run into quite a few designers who left this job to someone else, be it a client rep or an art director. I've also seen my share of studios where the designer wasn't given the opportunity to sell their own work, which is amazingly shortsighted. Selling your work directly to clients is extremely important. Not only should you be able to explain why you made the decisions you did, but you'll get first-hand feedback on where the work needs to go next.

How often has your work come back to you with changes you didn't understand or agree with? And all you had was a second-hand account of what was said, or worse yet, no explanation for why those changes were requested.

Once you are ready to take the responsibility for selling your work (and I am very purposefully using the word "selling," not "presenting") then you can begin to call yourself a designer. And get the credit for the good work you do.

A DESIGNER IS A GATEKEEPER

At some point in the next few days you will finish this book and I want you to immediately pick up Victor Papanek's *Design for the Real World,* which I will bluntly summarize like so: you are responsible for the work you put into the world.

Carefully choose the projects you take on. Choose to leave the world better than you found it. Improve things for people. This doesn't mean just working on non-profit or purely mission-driven projects. A lot of commercial products and services improve life for people in large and small ways. Just make sure there is some meaning to what you are doing besides exploiting a niche. Be the advocate for the person who will ultimately buy, use, or experience what you are designing.

We have limited resources, whether natural, financial, or cognitive. Don't contribute to people wasting them on crap.

You have more power than you think. And you are part of a long lineage of designers who fought to be listened to and respected. Designers like Victor Papanek, Tibor Kalman, Ray and Charles Eames, William Caslon, Paula Scher, Zuzana Licko, and our own Jeffrey Zeldman. Not only can a designer change the world, a designer *should.* This is the best job in the world! Let's do it right.

IN SUMMARY

Your toolbox should contain tools for input (goals and research), activity (make things!), and output (sell those things!). A designer's work starts way before a single pixel gets placed and ends way after the last one is locked in place. You may not take the lead in every, or even any part of the process; throughout your career you'll work on small teams, big teams, and sometimes alone. But even when you don't own a particular process, make sure to (respectfully) insert yourself. The more you know, the better your work will be. And don't wait to be asked.

2 GETTING CLIENTS

THE BIGGEST LIE in this book would be if I told you I don't worry about where the next client is coming from. I could tell you that once you build up enough of a portfolio, or garner enough experience, or achieve a certain level of notoriety in the industry, this won't be a concern anymore. I could tell you I sleep soundly, not bolting out of bed at 4 a.m. to run laps around the local high school track. I could tell you that I never worry about enough presents under the tree. I could tell you these things, but I'd be lying. And I don't want to lie to you. Getting clients is the most petrifying and scary thing I can think of in the world. I'd rather wrestle lady Bengal tigers in heat with meat strapped to my genitals than look for new clients.

If putting in the work to get the kind of work you want to do sounds too daunting, then close this book right now. Walk away. Rethink your life choices and take up a less stressful craft, like cleaning out cobra pits. Do it. No one will think less of you. Cover yourself in sackcloth and pray to your god for penance.

Go!

(Are they gone? Great! More clients for the rest of us.)

All kidding aside, getting clients can be one of the most daunting challenges a designer faces. After all, until you've actually secured a client, you can't do the job. That said, the biggest sure-fire way to not get clients is to be worried and freaked out. Clients are looking for confidence when they hire. You wanna make sure you don't land a client? Then act freaked out and worried. I'm not saying play "hard to get." I'm telling you to behave like someone who I'd entrust writing a large check to while putting my professional reputation in your hands.

This chapter will be of the most immediate use to freelancers and principals of moderately-sized shops. However, the concepts will be useful to anyone. Even if you're not in client services, or you're deep within the bowels of a large client services shop where clients just "happen," it's useful to know where they come from.

Clients are the lifeblood of a healthy business. They are the oxygen in your bloodstream that keeps everything going. No matter how good you are at what you do, without someone willing to pay you for that service you will have to close your doors. Lack of clients is the number one reason design studios fail. The number two reason? Who cares.

So where do clients come from? The best ones come one way.

REFERRALS

At this point, all of our jobs come through referral. Often, there is no formal RFP (request for proposal) process. In the case of some of the largest, best projects we've worked on, we weren't bidding against anybody else.

When you need a new doctor, lawyer, or butcher, your first inclination will always be to ask someone you trust. You value the opinions of people you trust, and it's faster than doing a lot of research on your own.

Say you wake up tomorrow morning with a weird pain in your knee (probably from doing laps at 4 a.m.). You'll make a mental run through your address book until you think of a friend who had knee problems last year. The next time you see her you'll ask her about the doctor who treated her, and after confirming she's not walking with a limp, you'll get that doctor's number. Now you not only have a doctor in mind, but you've gone from wondering if you can find a good doctor to hoping this particular doctor has an opening for you. All because of the wonderfully transitive properties of trust.

So it goes with hiring for design. Most people don't hire designers very often. (The average person's address book should contain more tailors than designers.) So during those odd times someone needs to buy design they'll confer with friends or colleagues who've hired designers in the past. And they'll certainly trust those referrals more than a Yelp listing or some unknown replying to a public RFP.

If you're trying to decide between two design firms that seem equally talented, the one that came with a referral has a solid advantage. And that vetting goes both ways—a client who is well-socialized and has a good reputation in a large network is more likely to be a great client. In most cases, you're going to be as skeptical of a client who hires a designer from an ad as they are of the designer who answered that ad.

How to get referrals

Most referrals come from colleagues or friends of colleagues, friends, or past clients. The keys to getting those referrals are:

1. Be pleasant to work with.
2. Do good work.

Get to know the people on the client team and treat them well. Make them a valuable part of the project and make sure their voices get heard. People change jobs. If the current project goes well, the person who hired you will have her stock rise within the company, and the rest of the staff will eventually spread out far and wide to other companies who will need design services at some point. Your DNA travels with them. (Not literally. I'm hoping I don't need to add a chapter explaining that.) When the call goes out to find a design partner, they'll be throwing your name in the ring.

Everything you deliver on a current project and every interaction you have with a current client is business development. All successful jobs lead to more jobs. And you are never not trying to line up your next job.

Be pleasant, don't be nice

We once received a call from a gentlemen who said, "[redacted] referred me to you. He said that you wouldn't be shy about telling me I was wrong, you'd probably piss me off, and that I should listen to everything you said because it would work."

I was delighted.

That said, you should aim to be pleasant to work with, as everyone would rather work with someone pleasant than with an asshole. But no one wants to work with someone who's faking it. Doing good work often requires a few hard conversations.

There's a difference between being enjoyable to work with and being "nice." Being nice means worrying about keeping up the appearance of harmony at the expense of being straightforward and fully engaged. Sometimes you need to tell a client they're making the wrong call. Part of client services is being able to do that without coming off as a dick. But being afraid to do it because you're too invested in being "nice" is worse than being a dick.

No one is hiring you to be their friend. They're hiring you to design solutions to problems. But if they can get the same solution from someone who's pleasant and someone who's a jerk, they'll go with the former.

Do good work

Of course, being the most pleasant person in the world won't help your cause if the work isn't good. But don't make the mistake of thinking the quality of your work by itself will be a shining beacon that pulls clients near. Good work is the core of your business, and for the purposes of this particular book let's assume you do good work. But clients aren't hiring your portfolio, they're hiring you. So while your portfolio is important as proof that you can do what you say you can (especially if you can match the work up with success metrics!), it can't be your biz dev department. You need to convince your potential clients that you'll be able to solve their problem as well as you solved your past clients' problems.

To do this design thing right we're going to have to redefine what we think of as "our work." That stuff in your portfolio? That's just evidence of work. The *real* work is that plus all the conversations, decisions, and convincing you did along the way.

Be clear (and enthusiastic) about what you do

Some people call this the elevator pitch. It's actually the standing-around-at-drinks pitch. (No one wants to make small talk in an elevator. Creepy and invasive.) You need to be able to explain what you do very succinctly and in an interesting manner. Everyone hates being cornered at a party by the guy who drones on about his work.

But if you sound really excited and confident about what you do when someone inquires in a perfunctory manner at a baby shower—and then you shut up—the person you are talking to might actually remember and recommend you when the occasion arises. This actually happens all the time.

Network

Research is a fundamental part of design. Networking is just research plus manners. In all of human history from the time your choice of careers was either hunting or gathering, it has never been easier to figure out who is in a position to hire you, and then figure out who you know who knows that person.

For an easier time doing this, it helps to know a lot of people.

If you are not a networking natural, try a user-centered approach, just like in design. Whenever you meet someone, start by learning something about them. Try to find out just a bit about what interests and motivates them. Try to think of something you could do to help them, whether it's validating their needs and interests or providing some useful information. Then when you talk about what you do, and what you need, just put it in that context.

This all has to come from a place of genuine interest and confidence. Or you risk sounding like a creepy stalker. As with all things, practice.

Don't be afraid to ask people you know for recommendations and referrals. Knowing someone to recommend is very exciting for people. Whether it's being thought of as karma or scoring business points, people love giving out referrals when they truly believe the person they're recommending is solid and trustworthy.

Be visible

A very wise (and handsome) man once told me, "No one's going to know what you think about unless you write and publish your opinions." I was incredibly shy and insecure about my writing when he said that. (Here's a secret: you don't get over it. You push through it.) Yet I knew that for the sake of my business I had to take that advice to heart. And you should too. People need to know who you are so they can write you checks. Write! Design! Put yourself out there. Let history decide whether it's crap or not. But unless you're putting yourself where people can see you and making your opinions known, clients or potential employers won't be able to find you. And the more you write the better you'll get at it. (Case in point, I'm almost certain the end of this book will be good.)

By the way, that very wise man started a publishing empire a few years later. Thanks, Zeldman.

Maintain relationships

The end of a project is not the end of the client relationship. First, you have a responsibility to check in on the success of the work. Were the longer-term goals met? Did the metrics meet everyone's expectations? Second, maintaining relationships is the single most important thing you can do to ensure good referrals. Not only did you nail the work, but you were pleasant while doing so and have remained pleasant afterward. You're a good person to know! And everyone wants to introduce good people to other good people.

Maintaining a relationship is not hard. (If my therapist is reading this I just screwed myself.) You're both busy people with sites to build and lives to live, so don't reach out with chores for them to do. Send the occasional email, or make the occasional phone call, to just say hello. Check in briefly. If their company just did something awesome send them an email, mention it on Twitter, and congratulate them publicly. Maybe once in a blue moon make plans for a drink or a meal. And yes, make sure to tell them you're always on the lookout for any referrals they can send your way, but don't make that the central point of conversation.

Reflect well on people who recommend you

When a friend or colleague recommends you to a potential client, you carry a responsibility to that referrer. You need to do right by them. They've put their reputation on the line to vouch for you. Treating that referral well not only shows that you're a reliable person, it also grows your referral network by one more happy client.

Sloppy work on your part reflects badly on the person who recommended you as well. Not only are you less likely to get another lead from that person, you might not be able to use them as a reference, and you've potentially added strife to the relationship between two of your clients.

Do you have to take a job that came from a referral? No. You still need to go through your process of deciding whether the client is right for you or not (coming up). But how you handle the inquiry is key. I'll give you an example.

We're a small shop. There are twelve of us as of this typing. And we get a fair amount of business inquiries. (Knock on wood. I love you all.) But we're not always the right studio for those jobs, and the faster we determine that, the better for everyone.

I need to manage the percentage of time I spend talking to leads versus the percentage of time I spend working with the clients to whom I've already made commitments. So meeting with every person who contacts us, as much as I might want to, would leave me little time to take care of current clients.

To help with this, we've developed a set of questions, a screener, to help both parties decide whether we're right for the job. If the potential project passes the initial screening, then we know it makes sense to devote some precious, otherwise billable time to pursue it. Some of the questions are common to all design studios: goals and necessary capabilities, timeline, and budget. There are several others we have added over the years as we've learned what qualities make a better or worse project for us.

(I love you guys so much I'll even give you link to the screener: http://muledesign.com/designbook/screener.html.)

The most important thing to keep in mind is that you are evaluating the potential client as much as they are evaluating you. Prospective clients sometimes find this surprising. Those folks aren't likely to make good clients.

As soon as we know that we're not the right studio for someone, we tell them. But a potential client who comes in from a referral is generally sent to us by someone who's worked with us before and thinks we're a good fit to solve this problem, so we're more inclined to sit down with them right away. After an initial conversation, we may in fact decide we're not a good fit after all, but we're going to do our best to refer them to someone who might be a better fit. We like them to leave feeling satisfied and helped. And someday they may have a project we'll be right for. So even when you choose not to work with someone you want to leave them with a good impression. If you give them a clear, positive idea of what you do, they will then refer you to others.

Referrals are the one true path. But surely there are others, right? Well, sure. There are also other tablets besides iPads, I suppose.

OTHER, LESS GOOD, WAYS TO GET WORK

First of all, before we go too far with the joke, these are all good things to be doing regardless. Although ninety percent or more of your work will come in through referrals, there's no reason to sit on your hands waiting for the phone to ring. Let's review some of these.

Request for proposals (RFPs)

There are many good organizations that have to go through an RFP process to hire anyone. And those are good jobs to go after. People who tell you they don't go after RFPs and people who tell you they don't have meetings are both lying to you. The problem with most RFPs is that they're written by people who are as irritated that they have to write it as you are that you have to reply to it.

That's also the key to handling an RFP. Find out who wrote it. Most come with a contact number in case you have questions. Call it. Make friends with the people who wrote it. They may have even heard of you. If so, you're golden. Strike up a conversation with them and get as much detail as you can about the organization involved.

The other problem with RFPs is that they can be overly prescriptive in nature. They can include specific solutions that may or may not be appropriate. This is usually an indication that the organization is freaked out about having to hire designers and is trying to maintain as much control as possible—to the point where they're going into as much detail as possible and short-circuiting the entire design process. You may be able to help them through that.

If an RFP starts dictating button colors, pick up the phone. It's a cry for help and your opportunity to create mutual understanding. Speaking directly to a designer may be what they need, much more than getting 325 replies to a badly-formed RFP. Remember, not all organizations who send out formal documents have to.

By the way, how do these organizations decide where to send these RFPs? By referral. BAM!

Outbound contact

I totally encourage you to go after clients you want to work for. Let's just be realistic about the return on this type of business development. It is very, very low. You're basically throwing seeds across a cement lot in the hope that one or two of them will find a crevice with enough dirt to take root in, not get eaten by birds, and that it'll rain at some point. It's hard enough to get a job that exists, but contacting people when a job may not exist is rough.

That said, if there's a client you're really interested in working with, go after them. Your best bet, as always, is going in through your network. Someone you know will know someone at that organization. Get ready to buy some meals and drinks. This is a little like that game where you start off with a paperclip and have to trade your way up to a dream client in ten moves or less. But with a little luck you may be able to get in front of the right people. More likely than not you'll be making a pitch to be considered should they have design needs in the future, so make a lasting impression. Pee in their fireplace or something.

Oh, and potential clients love getting cold calls as much as you do.

Advertising

We were once asked to co-sponsor a party at SXSW. I believe it was about three or four grand to get our name on the banner outside the bar and a listing in the program. We didn't have a spare three or four grand sitting around at the time. Instead we got stickers with our logo on them. Cost: $50. (It helps that our logo is an animal. People like animals.) We went to the party and gave everyone a sticker. People got drunk, put stickers on each other, took pictures, and uploaded them to the internet. You know how people referred to that party? The Mule party.

So yeah, I believe in advertising. I also believe in not throwing money away. Did we get any clients out of that party? Probably not, but we raised our profile a little bit. And we were only out $50. Oh, and we drank the free beer paid for by the people who anted up the $4K.

So host the occasional party, buy the occasional ad in a conference brochure. Be visible in places where clients look. Very targeted advertising might be helpful to raise your profile and let people know you exist, but I wouldn't put more than one or two eggs in this basket if you're trying to get clients. At the most, advertising might help you seem familiar to a potential client who's just been referred to you.

Conferences

Conferences are a fine place to meet both potential clients and peers. Sometimes these are the same person. They're full of other designers who work at organizations big enough to have a conference-going budget. (They're also more likely to expense dinner for a whole table, so tag along.) Those are the same large organizations who hire outside designers, and send out RFPs, at which point having someone on the inside will be invaluable.

Blog about things you want to work on

If you're interested in working with Disney, then blog about Disneyland. Write the best blog about Disney design on the internet. Will this in and of itself guarantee that you'll be the designer they call when they need work? No, but it certainly won't hurt. And you'll be writing about what you love anyway.

As always, the key to everything, especially getting clients, is confidence. No one wants to deposit a check into an ATM machine that looks like it just got wheeled in place yesterday and may not be there tomorrow. Ultimately you need to evaluate whether a client is the right client for you, because the perfect client is one that understands and values what you do, whose design problem plays to your strengths, and whose timeline matches your availability.

And this will keep the tigers away from your genitals.

3 CHOOSING THE RIGHT CLIENTS

GETTING CLIENTS IS GREAT. But they tend to come in enough different shapes and sizes that some of them will not be right for you. Or you may not be right for them. For the sake of both your businesses you need to make sure you're selecting the right clients.

You have a responsibility to your potential client to make sure you're actually the right designer for the job, and you have a responsibility to yourself to make sure the work you're bringing in is within your capabilities. If you're responsible for bringing in work for a shop full of people, you certainly have a responsibility not to put them in a bad position by bringing in work that doesn't play to their strengths.

The clients you choose to take on define you. Your portfolio needs to tell a story and each client you add to it is another chapter in that story. Make sure you're consciously building the story you want to be telling. And make sure your story is compelling enough that your next client is excited to become a character in it.

In ten years of business at Mule, we've taken on projects we've been personally excited about, projects we thought had a fantastic benefit to the world, projects we thought were great fun, projects with subject matter we were curious about, and yes, even projects that were taken primarily to keep the lights on (if any clients are reading this please rest assured that yours did not fit into that last category). But we've never taken on a project that we either were ashamed of or knew would be doomed from the start.

CAN YOU DO GOOD WORK FOR THIS CLIENT?

The business development process should go both ways. A potential client is trying to decide whether they want to work with you, and you're trying to decide whether you want to work with them. Are they tackling a problem that's interesting to you? Do you have the core competencies to solve it? Is there room for you in the problem-solving process? Can they pay you?

Over the years the one constant that we've been able to rely on is that how a potential client behaves in the business development process is *exactly* how they will behave during the project. Trust your gut. If they're slow to return your calls now, while they're trying to engage you, they'll be just as slow later. If gathering requirements or technical constraints is hard, then gathering feedback will be just as hard, if not harder. If your conversations reveal a May Day parade of red flags, then disengage. You will not be able to do good work, and neither you nor the client will be well-served.

Optimally, a client shows up and says, "We have a good sense for our problem, we're not tied to any particular solution, and we're looking forward to working together to come up with one using our collective expertise." And then we all take off on our unicorns. More likely than not, clients tend to show up with a solution in mind, even if they can't fully articulate the problem.

It's whether you're able to walk them backward from the solution they envision to the problem, and how open they are to that process, that lets you know they're going to be a good client. Your ability to do that is a sign of how good a designer you are as well.

That conversation generally goes something like this:

"The home page just needs two big buttons: 'buy pants' and 'subscribe to our newsletter about pants.'"

"What's your goal with those big buttons?"

"We want people to buy our pants."

"Are they good pants?"

"They're the best pants."

"Why don't we start by getting people as excited about your pants as you are?"

"Go on..."

That's gonna be a good client.

A bad client conversation goes like this:

"The home page just needs two big buttons: 'buy pants' and 'subscribe to our newsletter about pants.'"

"What's your goal with those big buttons?"

"What do you care? Just make my buttons!"

Bad client. Walk away and let them see how great you look in your pants as you do so.

DO THEY UNDERSTAND WHAT YOU BRING TO THE TABLE?

"Don't worry. We know exactly what we need."

Beware of clients who have waited to call you until they have a perfect diagram of what they need and want you to color it in. If they're not coming to you for strategy and problem-solving, they're not coming to you for design, they're coming to you for production. And if you take on production work, you don't get to call yourself a designer. (Yes, there's a union. And we're vicious.)

Look for clients who have clear goals, not detailed punch lists. This is especially true of RFPs that require you to reply directly to each line item at the risk of being disqualified from the process. You don't want to sign up for a process that you know is broken from the start. Once you set sail on a boat you can't convince a captain to take to the sky.

From a client's point of view, hire a designer to help you get to a solution. Not to execute on one. You wouldn't show up at a database analyst's door with a fully realized database schematic. Don't show up at a designer's door with a drawing of a tuna can.

BEWARE OF NEGGING

You know that douchebag at the bar who walks up to your friends and says, "You know, I usually date models...." Yeah, that guy. The client services version of that is, "You know, we've got some really big name agencies who'd love to get this job." Great, go call them. Don't work for someone who tries to make you feel they're lowering themselves to work with you, even as a negotiation tactic. Good work comes from mutual respect.

RELUCTANT BUYERS

Never work with someone who shows up begrudgingly and doesn't understand the value of design. It's not going to work out. If someone doesn't understand the value of what you do they're going to be reluctant to both pay the price and do the work to get it done right.

We see this with early stage startups who were sent by their VCs. They don't want to be working with a design agency. Either they don't see the value, or they feel like bringing in an outside resource is slowing them down. We also see it with internal designers who were sent by a higher-up. Sometimes they feel like they should have been allowed to do the job themselves, sometimes they're freaked out about their own job security. Either way, a reluctant buyer will be focused on proving that you weren't needed and trying to disengage themselves from the process like a little kid tanking the violin lessons his dad forced him to take.

The design process gets messy, and people need to be able to tell each other difficult things like "Your business model won't work." You won't be able to have those discussions with people who don't value what you have to say.

IS THIS PROJECT CORE TO THEIR BUSINESS?

Someone who is in the business of selling pants will still be selling pants in three to four months, provided they're still selling anything. But when someone selling pants comes to you with an idea to sell toasters, beware. Why are they getting into a new business? Is it a natural growth of their existing business? Does their expertise in their current business translate to their new business? Or is it an opportunistic attempt to "fill a hole in the market"? That hole may close before the project is over, and they'll want to move to the next opportunity. Want to redo all that work? No, because they'll want you to do it for free.

Which brings us to the most important thing of all.

WORK FOR MONEY

You are in business. You need to be as confident about money as you are about design.

How clients talk about money is also a good indication of what sort of client they will be. Do they already have the money? Do they have to make the business case for design to get the money? What do they value and what are they willing to pay for? What don't they want to pay for? Do they have access to as much money as it will take? Do they already have a budget limit? Have they already worked with a designer who took their money and didn't give them value in return? Are they cagey about telling you how much they want to spend? If so, why?

Beware of clients who want you to work for equity or other things that can't be easily converted into rent. There's too much there beyond your control. And especially beware of clients who tell you the work you do together will look great in your portfolio. For one, it probably won't. A client who asks you to work for less than market rates already disrespects you. How do you think that'll play out during the project? Think you're getting portfolio-level work out of that? Secondly, you're in business to make money. I'm lucky enough that I get to do what I love, but only because I can make a living off of it. Working for portfolio fodder is the same as dying young and leaving a good-looking corpse.

Never work for free. Any work you take on for free will get pushed aside for paying work. That does neither you nor the client any favors. Neither of you will respect each other's time. If the situation merits it, work at a discounted rate. But submit a budget showing the actual rate, with the discount applied. Let the client know the value of what they're getting.

Money is a standard part of any business transaction. Watch out for clients who don't understand the financial value of what they're hiring you for. In ninety-five percent of the jobs we've taken on, our clients have met or exceeded their success metrics after our work was done. Can we take full credit for that? Sure! Well, no, probably not, but it's safe to say we were definitely a part of it. Design, done right, is not a loss on the balance sheet and should not be bought or sold as one. Design is an investment in infrastructure and keeps the wheels of business running smoothly. Good design equals a more effective product or service. Design equals profit!

YOUR ROLE IN MAKING CLIENTS BETTER

Now, it's easy to laugh at clients and say they're bad clients. But the truth is that no one is born knowing how to be a good client, just as no one is born knowing how to be a good designer. And look how hard you have to work at being a good designer!

By and large, most clients want to be good clients, and they're trying to do the right thing by their business.

Clients will always ask you to make their logo bigger, prescribe solutions, and ask you to do things that will make you smack your forehead. You can roll your eyes at how much they don't understand about design or you can roll up your sleeves and begin practicing your craft by helping them clarify what they need.

Not knowing the design language doesn't make someone a bad client. I doubt very much that most of you could have a medical conversation with your doctor on par with a conversation your doctor could have with another doctor, and that doesn't make you a bad patient. And just like a good doctor can put you at ease with a sensitive bedside manner and care with professional terminology, so must a good designer cultivate a productive means of getting the necessary information from their clients.

It's your job as a designer, and a communication professional, to find the right language to communicate with your client. When you say a client doesn't "get it" you might as well be saying, "I couldn't figure out how to get my point across. I am a lazy designer. Please take all my clients from me."

YOUR ETHICAL RESPONSIBILITY

You have a responsibility to the community at large to make sure that what you're signing up to design is worth being designed. That's right, kids: I'm interjecting ethics into the mix. You are responsible for the work you put into the world.

A few years ago I was interviewing a designer for a job. We ended up passing on him. Not because the work was bad; it wasn't. And not because he interviewed badly; he didn't. We passed on him because, while reviewing his portfolio, we came across work for a client I won't name. Let's just say their product kills people.

"Why did you work on that?" I asked.

There are two answers I would have accepted from him. "I don't have a problem with their business model—in fact, I think there are too many people in the world." Weird? Sure. But hey, he would have been taking a stand. The second answer I'd have accepted would've been, "They're terrible, but I really needed the money and had no other options." I can't begrudge anyone making a living, and we've all done a few things we're not proud of.

Instead he looked surprised that I was asking the question and said something to the effect that it was just the next project on his plate.

I asked him if he agreed with how the client made their money. He replied in the negative—he'd just done the design. I told him we didn't take on any projects that we couldn't ethically stand behind.

And here I'll quote him: "Must be nice."

And that's when I decided not to hire him.

Now, I'm not trying to embarrass this individual, who I'm sure will have a solid design career, and I might have even done the same thing at his age. But as a designer, hell, as *any* type of craftsperson, you are responsible for what you put into the world. You are defined by the clients you take on, and you can only stand as proud of the work as its benefit to society entitles you to.

So before you take on a client, ask yourself whether the problem the client is asking you to solve is one you feel good about attaching your name to. Are they serving a real need? There is absolutely nothing wrong with making money—in fact, one of the goals of this book is to encourage you to make your fair share—but making it to someone else's detriment makes you complicit in that person's downfall. If a product you design does harm, then you have done harm.

I urge each and every one of you to seek out projects that leave the world a better place than you found it. We used to design ways to get to the moon; now we design ways to never have to get out of bed. You have the power to change that.

MAKING IT WORK

Client services is a story based on a series of good relationships. Before you enter into one make sure that all the necessary elements for success are there. You'll be spending some time with these people, and both your reputations are on the line.

Make sure you can spot the differences between a client who needs your help, an otherwise good client who's just not a good fit for you, and an actual bad egg.

Will following these rules help you get better clients? Probably. Are they fail-safe? Oh, hell no. But they're based on many, many years of trial and error, messing up, dusting myself off, and trying again. As always, I'm not advocating for a single way of getting real or getting things done; I'm telling you how it worked out for me. Your mileage will certainly vary. Above all, the best advice I can give you in selecting your clients is to be confident, treat everyone with the same respect you want them to treat you with, trust your gut, and iron your shirt.

Now that we've decided who to work with let's figure out what to charge them.

4 CHARGING FOR YOUR WORK

THIS SHOULD BE the shortest chapter of the book. Anything I have to tell you can be summed up thusly: charge as much as you can, deliver an honest value, and never work for free. Unfortunately, most designers feel such pangs of guilt about charging an adequate amount for their work, if anything at all, that it's probably worth the time and effort to go a little deeper.

LET'S GET COMFORTABLE TALKING ABOUT MONEY

Before we go any further we need to get over this money thing. It has come to my attention that some of you are uncomfortable with the idea of money. Let's start by going over a short list of people who are *not* uncomfortable with money: your landlord, your utility companies, your insurance agent, your grocer, your tailor (yes, you should have one), and your doctor. If you have kids, let's add their orthodontist and the bursar at their eventual college of choice to the list. Money is so necessary to the fabric of society that even my friends in Berkeley have a secret guilty stash of it.

The minute you got into the design game, you took up a trade that involves money changing hands. And hopefully you can get on the receiving end of that transaction. You are not *doing* design, you are *selling* design, which is a valuable service. If you don't want to charge for your services, you can pick up *Design Is a Hobby* on aisle three of Michael's between the balsa wood and yarn.

But if you are trying to make a living as a designer, then comfort with money needs to be part of your skill set. There will be no "ums," no hesitation when a client asks for a price, no asking them to tell you what your work is worth. As with all parts of the job, confidence begets confidence, and it's even more so with money. No one wants to hand money to someone who behaves like they don't deserve it, or has no idea what to do with it.

And above all, you will never, ever tell a client, "I'm not comfortable talking about money."

My friend Anil Dash once said that if you hand a client an estimate and slap them across the face and they complain about the slap, then the estimate wasn't high enough. The best part is that he was actually a client when he said that.

So how much should you charge? You charge as much as you can. If you can stand in front of a client completely confident and explain why you are worth the amount you quoted, you should charge it. The problem with designers isn't that they don't know how much to charge; it's that they're afraid to charge it!

You can always negotiate down from a price that was too high, but you can't recover from a price that was too low. You're stuck with that. There is nothing wrong with trying to get the highest price for your work. It's supply and demand. The more demand there is for a particular service, the more suppliers of that service can charge. You'll find that your rates will fluctuate as the market for design ebbs and flows. But if you are not confident in the value of your work, there's no way you'll be comfortable charging a fair price.

APPROACHING PRICING

A few years ago I was fortunate enough to work with a company called Kickstart (not to be confused with Kickstarter, the excellent crowd-sourcing project funding service). Kickstart is an NGO (non-governmental organization) that designs and manufactures low-cost water pumps for use in impoverished agricultural areas of the world, mainly in Eastern Africa. They have an amazing track record of helping people lift themselves out of poverty by using these simple, easy-to-fix water pumps to irrigate crops. They create jobs. Here's why I'm mentioning it: they don't give away the pumps, like most NGOs would. They sell them.

The Kickstart founders spent years working with NGOs who donated equipment and tools to those in need, only to return to the scene and find that the equipment had been scavenged for parts or was sitting unused and rusting away. People didn't value (or need) what they had been given. So Kickstart decided to sell their pumps, marketing them as the "Super MoneyMaker." The results were impressive. Instead of free hand-outs, the Super MoneyMaker became an item the poorest people in the world would save up for. Only people who actually planned to use one would buy one. When you pay for something with your own money, you value it more than when you get it for free. You take care of it. Most telling, people would scavenge from other things to repair their Super MoneyMakers.

Undercharging for your work has the same effect. You're telling your client the work has little value. Clients value you in direct proportion to how much it costs them. If you have ever done volunteer work, you may have noticed that the people you were volunteering for had no trouble making increasing demands on your time. No one is going to value your work, or your time, if you don't.

Oh, and guess how much people value free work? You got it.

Your design work is your client's Super MoneyMaker.

WHAT TO CHARGE

About once a week we get an email or call that starts, "How much do you charge for a website?" And while it's easy to roll your eyes at a question like that, you'd do better to remember two things: you're in a service profession, and it's actually a fair question. From a client's perspective, the basis for pricing is opaque at best.

Design can mean a lot of things. Ask five designers what they would charge to design the exact same thing and you will get five different answers. To a prospective client, the idea of hiring a design firm can be daunting enough without having to figure out how much it's all going to cost. Calling a bunch of design firms and getting a range of prices that don't resemble each other has got to make you feel like people are just making this shit up. Which they are.

A client can get work of any description for a cost between zero and infinity. And people who don't buy design every day might not have a good idea of all the options that go into setting a price. It's your job to help them figure it out. And sometimes the best way to do that is to help them map it to something they are familiar with purchasing. After all there's not much difference between asking, "How much do you charge for a website?" and "How much do you charge for a car?" Except that people have probably bought a car before. They know that the type of car a college student needs to get back and forth to class is vastly different than what parents with a new set of twins need. And that they'll have to pay more for the latter. And that, even among one type of car, the price can vary wildly based on their quality and feature set, which really isn't that different from decisions you'd have to make in choosing what kind of website you want and who you want to build it. Except they may not know that yet (metaphors are handy).

When you first go off on your own to freelance, or start a studio, you might have the idea that everyone else has it all figured out. (We totally do! I'm totally lying!) There's no secret formula for knowing how much to charge for your work. There's only the experience you gain from having to do it over and over again. You'll undercharge a few; you might even overcharge a few. But eventually you do it enough times that patterns start to emerge. You gain enough experience to realize that this new job is similar to a job you did last year, which you undercharged for. So you make the correction. Eventually what you gain is the confidence to trust your math and the experience to trust your instincts.

If you're ever in a situation where you can overhear a couple of design studio heads having a casual conversation, try to listen in. The way each maneuvers to get the other to reveal their pricing structure is as fascinating as watching two overweight old bulldogs in the dog park circling each other for a genital sniff, but with much less probability of success. And a lot more slobber.

The going rate for design work isn't posted anywhere like the price of apples. And unlike competing grocers, you can't casually walk by their apple stand and see what your competition is charging to adjust your prices accordingly. But with a little savvy and a bit of friendliness you should be able to get a general idea, at least a ballpark hourly rate, of what others are charging. Decide who you are competing against, and you will at least have a good ballpark to start playing in.

There is always someone cheaper. Negotiate price, but don't compete on price. Compete on quality, value, and fit.

Charge for value, not time

There are formulas that claim to help you figure out what to charge by looking at how much you need to make. They'll have you add up your expenses, rent, supplies, utilities, etc., and then add a markup to that based on how much profit you want. But there's a problem with most of those formulas: they do not calculate a billing rate—they calculate a cover-your-ass rate. You should, of course, know the minimum rate you need to make to keep the lights on. But you should be charging clients based on what that work is worth to them, not the time it takes you to complete it.

Let's say you're working on bids for two logos for the same company. One is a logo for an internal project team. The other is for a new service they're expecting to become a major new profit center. And let's also say you expect both of them to take you the same amount of time. (Bear with me as I over-simplify the hell out of this.) Are you going to charge the same for both? No, you are not. Because the first logo is designed to build camaraderie around an internal project, while the second is part of a major project release that could stand to make the company a lot of money. It's got a much higher value to the company.

Only you know the value of your time. (Hint: it is greater than $0.) But the value of your work to a particular client depends on what the client has to gain from that work. And the client is not buying time from you. They are buying work. The value of that work is what you need to charge them for.

Do your research

This is different than the research you'll be doing once you sign the project. You get paid for that. This is research in support of putting together a smart bid.

Find out as much about the company you'll be working for as possible. Do they have a history of launching products on time? Is there a possibility that they'll be acquired or shut down during the project? Are you dealing with the actual decision-makers? Can you have access to the actual decision-makers? And the super obvious, but oft-forgotten: do they have money to pay you?

Find out about their internal teams and their involvement in the project. If they're responsible for major pieces (content strategy and the backend buildout are two excellent examples), have conversations with the people responsible for that. Make sure you'll all be speaking the same project language. (This also goes a long way toward building allies in the upcoming project, by the way.)

Do some research into the market landscape as well. Maybe there's a good reason why no one else has been able to sell mismatched socks online.

Not only will this research help you prepare a solid price, the knowledge you gain from it will make you a better salesperson. And help you to close the deal with confidence. (Or tell you enough to stay away from the project!)

Figure out what the client really wants early

Most clients will approach you with a wish list of desires. If they don't you should actually work with them on coming up with one. Assign a cost and a benefit to each one. Then figure out which ones are crucial to the project and which ones would be nice to have. Figure out which ones actually fit into their overall goals. Not only will this help you come up with a proper scope, but it'll give you a handy list of priorities should you need to adjust the budget. It also keeps additional things from popping up later in the project, you know, after it's been scoped.

Clearly define your services

Make sure the client knows exactly which services they are being charged for, and just as importantly, which ones they aren't being charged for. Explain how the services are inter-connected. For example, research isn't there to be cut; the rest of the work is actually contingent upon it. Show the client that you've thought through the different parts of a project and that each of those parts has a cost. You'd expect this kind of itemization from any other business, and design is no different. When your mechanic presents you with a bill, you may cringe; but when he goes over the itemized list you begin to see how that figure got there, and you see the care and concern that went into preparing that number. It also doesn't occur to you to talk your mechanic down because you can see that each part has a cost. Your job is to treat your time and expertise as if it has that same set cost.

We've also found that delivering a chart of all the steps necessary to the site launch with a column for what we're responsible for and what they're responsible for is a good way to find out what services the client may not even be aware they need. And, of course, we're talking about content migration. Of course we are.

"But it'll only take me an hour!"

Good for you! That should be a highly profitable job.

Don't punish yourself for being good or efficient. I've seen designers pull their hair out trying to solve something and I've seen designers nail something on the first try. Quite often these were the same designers on consecutive days. In either situation, what the client pays for is that solution, not the time it took you to get there. If it should take you less time than what was estimated and agreed to, and that estimate was created honestly based on previous similar work: great.

(I'll be honest with you. Because I love you and you're not going to share this with clients. I have actually sat on work for a few extra days and waited to deliver it closer to the estimated date just to avoid this conversation. But I'm a bad person. I'm certainly not recommending you do this.)

The flip side of that, of course, is that you can't charge the client for the time it takes you to learn a particular tool. If a client hired you to build something in a platform you don't know yet but feel confident you can learn, the time it takes you to pick up that expertise is on you. Once you consider yourself capable, turn the meter on.

Large jobs vs. small jobs

Beware of small jobs. The greatest trick the devil ever pulled was convincing the world that a small job wouldn't be too much of a problem.

When I was in college I took a holiday job loading UPS trucks at night. I trained with a guy named Frank. First piece of advice Frank gave me was, "Watch out for the small boxes, kid."

"Why?"

"You'll find out."

Sure enough, I absentmindedly grabbed the first small box that shot out of the chute and it slammed my hand into the floor. Frank laughed and laughed. He laughed even harder when he realized I needed stitches. I really liked Frank. (The box was filled with ball bearings, by the way.)

The moral of this story is that small jobs contain the same kinds of problems as big jobs, minus the budget and the time to deal with them adequately. You'll try to squeeze them into as little time as possible and they don't want to be squeezed. Remember, a small job for you is not necessarily a small job for the client. And while you may be thinking that this is a little something you can squeeze in between big projects, the client is still expecting the same amount of detailed attention you're giving your bigger projects. And they'd be right to expect that.

GETTING YOUR PRICE

Mention ballparks early to avoid sticker shock

As a kid I was lucky enough to be raised in the fine city of Philadelphia (holla!) and unlucky enough to witness baseball at Veterans Stadium (pronounced *VEH-tchrn*). Veterans Stadium was one of those terrible multi-use complexes built in the 70s that tarnished the landscape in several cities across America. Anyhow, as a kid I didn't have much money, so my friends and I would get seats in the 700 level, the highest level of the stadium. (Between pitches we'd throw batteries at the airplanes flying below us.)

This is an incredibly long-winded way to tell you that as soon as a client calls we try to give them what we call a "700 level ballpark figure." Meaning, we can't see too much of the detail on the field yet, but it sounds like it's an $80–$120K project. As we gain insight into the project we'll start getting more precise with that figure and communicate that with them so that by the time they get a proposal in front of them it's a figure they'll be prepared for.

If a potential client is going to have sticker shock, get it over with as soon as possible. Before you've taken the time to put together a proposal.

Nothing in your proposal should be a surprise

Some people treat proposals like they are passing a number in a folded piece of paper across a table to be peeked at and then accepted or rejected. Just as a design project requires client input and feedback along the way, so does a proposal. Start with a high-level draft and iterate quickly, with the client offering insight into anything that may trip up their team and pointing out potential roadblocks.

The frank and open communication you begin here will serve you well throughout the project. You need to expose all implicit assumptions because the road to feeling ripped off is paved with assumptions about what you were getting. You and the client may agree on a number and have radically different ideas of what that number includes.

It's perfectly fine to summarize what is included and what isn't for reference. Another way to handle this is to list everything that needs to be done on the project and who is responsible for it, whether it is you, the client, or a third (even as-yet-unnamed) party. You compile this list by means of a phone call or in-person conversation in which you go through the list of everything that you anticipate will need to be done and ask the client who they would like to be responsible for that work. Everything you are responsible for goes into your estimate. Everything you aren't responsible for goes on a list of scope exclusions.

Here is a short list of terrible surprises to avoid, just to give you an idea:

- Copywriting
- Backend development
- Localization
- Video production and motion graphics
- Custom illustration
- Content migration
- Print collateral
- CMS customization
- SEO
- Maintenance

Your personal charm and enthusiasm for your work should convert your main client contact into a strong ally by the time the proposal is finalized, so that you already have the blessing of a person on the inside when it's time to present the proposal.

Present it, don't send it!

Putting together a proposal can be such an onerous and time-consuming job that getting it all wrapped up can feel like a victory. And it is—of sorts. But you haven't won anything yet. Getting the proposal ready just means that you're now ready to sell it. It's really enticing to write a nice little email, attach the proposal, and ride off to the couch or bar. It's also a great way to lose a job.

Don't ever leave a proposal on its own. A proposal is a prop for a sales presentation. If at all possible, get yourself in front of the client's decision-makers and sell. Everything you learned while preparing the proposal should be at your disposal. Read the room. Go over as much or as little detail as the room requires. Make sure you go over key benefits of the proposal. You don't sell features, you build features. You sell benefits. You are convincing them to hire you, not accept your proposal. The proposal is merely one data point toward that decision. Your presentation skills will decide how big a data point it is.

Three things can happen now: you can not get the job, you can get the job right away, or you can be asked to negotiate. It's a little bit like the three bears. And guess whose porridge is just right? Getting the job right away? No.

"Why is your bid higher than the others?"

I love it when a client asks this question. You will learn to love it as well. First off, congratulations on having the confidence to bid high but not too high! Second, your high bid did not scare off the client. Furthermore, you're being presented with an excellent opportunity to further sell yourself. The client is asking you to close the deal.

You need to sound confident as hell that not only did you bid correctly, but that you are the best possible fit for this job. And by going into detail about how you got to that price, you can show them that you have a detailed understanding of what it will take to get that job done. Which, by the way, you better have.

Also, this is an opportunity to build yourself up, not tear others down. Don't badmouth other bidders; you're not helping yourself by doing that. Quite the opposite. You don't want to get a job because you convinced someone the other bidders sucked. You want to get the job because you were the right person for it.

Negotiation

Having to negotiate your price isn't a sign that something went wrong—it's a sign that something went right.

You will know you charged too little if the client agrees right away. There's nothing quite as disconcerting as seeing a client's eyes light up and their mouth turn into a Cheshire cat-like grin when they see your estimate and their pen races to sign the dotted line before you realize your mistake.

Ideally, your price should require a bit of negotiation. You don't want to charge so much that they don't feel like they can negotiate, but you also don't want to leave money on the table. You want a client to feel like your time and expertise are valuable, that you're right for the job, and that it may take a little work on everybody's part to make this happen. Once a client has decided to put effort into working together, they have skin in the game and it's in their best interest to get it to work.

If the client wants the price lowered, go over all the items in the proposal and find out what can be cut. Never lower the price without taking something away. And never take something away without explaining the lost benefit. If the lost benefit wasn't that great then maybe it's a fine thing to cut anyway. The amount isn't arbitrary; every item has a set cost. So if you want to pay less you have to be willing to get less.

And when I talk about things to cut I am talking about the amount of stuff the client will have delivered to them, i.e., site features. You can't cut parts of your process that you need to do the job. The answer to "Can we take out this research?" is always no.

Remember, the client wouldn't be negotiating with you if they didn't already want to work with you. So negotiate from a place of confidence. That means being okay with not getting the job. Confidence doesn't come from knowing you're right—it comes from being okay with failing.

Why clients think they can lowball

First off, let's define lowballing as the actions of a client who is not necessarily constrained by budget but wants to convince you that you should undercharge for your work. This is different from a client who values your work but is stuck with a fixed budget.

It's a client's job to get the most work from you for the least amount of money. And they're comfortable doing it because you probably presented the price in an apologetic tone with a lot of up-talking. We all know what up-talking is, right? It's when you end every sentence as if it were a question. Like you're asking for approval for what you just said. The next time you have dinner with a bunch of people pay attention to how they give the waiter their order.

"And for you, sir?"

"I'll have the pasta?"

Just once I'd like the waiter to come back with, "No. Actually, that was wrong. I've got you down for the fish."

Those are people who haven't clearly made up their mind about what they're having and defaulted to something they weren't totally sure about. It's easy to change their minds. So when you negotiate price with a client and say, "That'll be $50,000?" What they hear, if they're good at their job—which is to get the best value for the best price—is "I can totally be talked down to $40,000."

Clients may also lowball you because design doesn't hold any value for them. You should have weeded those clients out earlier, but they get through once in a while. If you're not delivering your estimate with confidence, you're reinforcing their opinion.

How can you prevent them from doing it? Well, present with confidence and conviction and back your numbers up with good solid research, of course. But more important than trying to prevent them from doing it is how to address it when it happens. Stand your ground. You gave your price. And like I said, it's their job to try to talk you down. They've got to try, right?

Get comfortable saying, "No." Go stand in front of a mirror right now. C'mon. Let's do it together. "No. This is my price. This is what it costs to work with me."

You will lose work. But you will also feel better about the work you get. You may even get a reputation as a hard-ass. I can tell you from personal experience, it's not the end of the world.

IN SUMMARY

Look, money is hard. It took me years to get comfortable with the idea of being a financial grownup. And I doubt many of you got into this business for the money. I'm guessing you're here because you love design. But to practice your craft you need to keep the lights on, and you need your financial house in order. The more attention you pay to this stuff at the right time, the less of your overall day you'll spend worrying and fretting about it. Don't worry about money, deal with money.

The secrets to getting the price you want for your work are having done the homework to know you're asking for the right thing, the confidence to ask for it, and the willingness to walk away when you can't get it. Now that I think of it, I just accidentally gave you the secret to life, which I was saving for another book.

5 WORKING WITH CONTRACTS

I'LL ASSUME THAT everyone reading this book was given "the talk" at some point during their passage through the sticky doors to adolescence. You know; *the* talk. Where one—or good grief, *both*—of your parents pulls you aside and attempts to talk to you about sex. And being safe. And respecting one another. And protection. And you're pretty sure they're more freaked out by giving the talk than you are of getting it.

Some of us, including me, have now had to give the talk to our own teenagers. (Any doubt I had about him being my kid vanished when he said, "Yeah, I already know all of this from 4chan.")

Talking to teens about sex is a lot like talking to designers about contracts. "We're being careful. We're in love. We trust each other. They have an agile process. He promised there wouldn't be any backend development."

A contract is like a prophylactic. It won't keep you from getting fucked, but it may keep you free from additional liabilities down the road.

See how I lured you into a chapter about contracts with tawdry sex talk? At the end of the chapter I'll tell you a great dirty joke, too.

In the last chapter we learned how to convince clients to work with us. Everything was great. We sold them on what a great partner we'd be; we were ready to start working; everyone was happy, etc., etc. Shouldn't we be designing by now? What went wrong?

Nothing. And we're going to do our best to keep it that way, by specifying the responsibilities of each party to the greatest extent possible in a written document signed by both parties.

WHY A CONTRACT?

A contract establishes the nature of the relationship between all parties and makes the important stuff clear to everyone involved:

- What are the ground rules for working together?
- How much money is exchanged and at what point?
- What are the deliverables, and when are they due?
- What happens if there is a delay?
- Who has what rights? What rights does the client get and when? Which do you retain?

And very importantly, a contract states what should happen if everything goes to hell. No one goes into a relationship with the intention to screw the other party, but things happen. Markets collapse. Funding falls through. Leadership changes.

Often, the problem is that one party assumed the other was responsible for something when this wasn't the case—something like a trademark search or content migration.

Then there are deadlines. They get missed on both sides. Do you want to be liable when your client is telling you they're going to miss the holiday shopping season because the site is late to launch?

You can prevent a lot of weirdness—expensive, painful weirdness—down the road if you clarify all this up front.

Getting entangled in ambiguity or dealing with a legal dispute keeps you from getting paid for your work, creates a huge amount of frustration, threatens your reputation (your most important asset), and keeps you from spending your day designing stuff.

In short, a contract is what you need to start building trust between all parties. No contract, no basis for trust.

GET A LAWYER (A LOVE STORY)

Many, many years ago when our company was still in its infancy we were working with a particular client on a website. And, yes, we had a contract in place, one we'd cobbled together from a combination of online resources and other design companies who'd been kind enough to share their contracts with us. The project was going well enough. Until it wasn't.

The client, for whatever reason, had decided he was dissatisfied with our design solutions. It happens. We work through it. Except this particular client decided to bring in another designer, someone he'd previously worked with on print collateral to design the site. Since the project was for a full build-out he expected us to take this other designer's work and build the site. (Small aside here: if anyone approaches you to work on a project they've already hired another designer for, walk away. Professional courtesy. More on that in Chapter 10.)

Our contract specifically stated that the client couldn't bring in another designer to do the work he'd hired us for. So we pulled him aside and talked to him about it. (Contract conversations should happen in person, if at all possible, and never in front of the whole team. Gives everyone a chance to save face.)

Unfortunately the client did not see it the way we did and threatened to sue us for refusing to finish the project. Not having been in business for very long, and not having huge reserves of cash, we freaked out. We'd never had a client threaten to sue us before! Several conversations with the client only seemed to make things worse.

We knew we needed a lawyer, and fortunately we remembered the name of the friendly corporate counsel from a previous employer. She recommended we call her partner's son, a smart young lawyer at a local firm. His name is Gabe.

Gabe listened to our story, looked over our contract, smirking while he read it, and said the most magical phrase I'd ever heard: "I can make this go away." And after a calm but forceful phone call, he did.

Sadly, we had to fire the client. (Yes, sadly. I take no pride in ever having to do that, and to this day we've only ever had to do it twice.) But we were able to walk away relatively unscathed, with a lesson learned.

Most importantly, we added a valuable member to our team: Gabe Levine is still with us to this day. He solidified all our standard contracts, reviews incoming contracts, gives us client relationship advice, and has even come on stage with me when I talk about contracts.

Why am I waxing so rhapsodic about my lawyer? He makes sure my contracts are strong and helps me negotiate with confidence. Having him as an advisor makes me confident enough in what I'm doing that I ask for what I'm worth and don't negotiate my rights away. But most of all, I love my lawyer because he makes me money.

By and large the first thing I hear when someone tells me they're having a problem getting paid and I tell them to hire a lawyer is, "They're too expensive." Yes, they *do* cost money. But so do you! The better our contracts, the more secure our client relationships. His job isn't to sue clients—it's to make sure we never land in a place where we *have* to. And ultimately he is trained and knowledgeable in things that I am not. Not having to do those things, and letting someone do them well, means I can spend my time doing what I'm good at—designing things. I happily write two checks every month. His is the first; my therapist's is the second.

The second comment I hear most about lawyers is, "Are things at the point where I need a lawyer already?" Things were at that point when you decided to stop being an amateur and turned pro. Look: you don't need to carry your lawyer around with you or talk to her every day. Work with her on a solid master contract to cover your most frequent needs, especially if you're a contractor or freelancer, and then get her on the phone if the client has questions about it.

How to introduce your client and your lawyer

For the most part your lawyer is an invisible advisor. She should review all of your contracts, but she rarely exposes herself to the client. This isn't to say that your lawyer needs to be a secret. In fact, you should make no bones about telling your client that you're having your lawyer review something. They are likely doing the same. Sometimes, as in the example above, just letting a client know that you have a lawyer as well helps to put them, well, let's say at *ease*.

There's nothing wrong with letting your lawyer and the client's lawyer settle small contract disputes directly. It usually saves a lot of time. Heck, they probably went to school together. But never, ever, and I mean *never* talk to a client's lawyer directly without yours present. Only lawyers talk to other lawyers. Sometimes negotiating a very large project requires a friendly conference call with everyone and their lawyers. You can accomplish in one hour what might take days exchanging tracked changes.

We've been on conference calls with clients and found out their lawyers were, unexpectedly to us, on the call as well. So we calmly stated, "Unfortunately, we're going to have to reschedule this call when our lawyer is available as well."

This can go one of two ways.

1. The client is upset you have a lawyer. This is a huge red flag. This is a business relationship and good business people keep a lawyer handy to make sure they don't do anything stupid.
2. Or, everyone is fine with it and you reschedule when your lawyer can join in.

Your lawyer is there to help you make sure you're in the best possible position to help your clients without putting yourself in a bad spot. Your lawyer is a defensive asset and not to be weaponized unless absolutely necessary. If you have a lawyer who is turning everything into a fight, then it's time for a conversation, or a new lawyer.

TALKING TO CLIENTS ABOUT CONTRACTS

If you're working with a large organization you may spend some time haggling about the contents of a contract, and they may even attempt to substitute their contract for yours. In either situation, you'll want to confer with your excellent lawyer. However, if you're working with a smaller organization, or even with an individual, they may balk at the idea of a contract at all. And just as it's your job to sell design, it may also become your job to sell them on the need to define the business relationship properly.

If a client flat-out refuses to sign a contract, that's a red flag. But don't give up right away: it may be that they're just uncomfortable with the idea and need to talk about it. You'll need to learn to make your case for why the contract is important to both of you, and be ready to walk away from the job should you be unable to convince them. A larger company may also refuse to sign your contract, and ask you to sign theirs instead. (They may refer to theirs as a "Master Services Agreement," the same way Swanson calls hamburger "Salisbury steak.") In which case you should run it by your lawyer before signing.

Contracts protect both parties

Every relationship you have has an implicit contract. For example, if your buddy calls you and tells you that he just got dumped it's implied that you will meet him at a bar right away. If your kid is sick it's implied that you'll make chicken soup. You hold the door open for the person behind you. You take turns merging into traffic. These are the implicit contracts that keep society moving along at a nice pleasant clip.

But what happens when these implicit contracts go wrong? Tension builds and, eventually, arguments arise because one party believed the other party was responsible for behaving a certain way. (This is why I had my lawyer draw up a contract between me and my kid.)

Having an explicit understanding of what is expected from both parties in a relationship—an explicit agreement of what happens should something go wrong—relieves that tension. People go into a business arrangement with the best of intentions and a lot of assumptions. A contract makes those assumptions explicit by documenting the terms of engagement clearly.

If any red flags or concerns come up during the business development process, make sure those are addressed in the contract. Unless they are so big and unresolvable that you need to walk away.

For example, let's say you've decided, for whatever reason, to work with a company that's just laid off a thousand employees. Make sure the contract addresses what happens should the team you're working with get laid off. And from the client's side: let's say they're worried about working with an agency that's out of state. Make sure a certain amount of visits to their office are baked into the contract.

That said, both parties don't necessarily need equal protection. It's doubtful that a 10-person studio, or one freelance designer, can bring down a startup of 100, much less an established multi-national corporation. Make sure your contract protects *you* adequately.

The larger and more established the organization, the more heinously skewed in their favor their terms are going to be. Always start from a strong position with your desired terms in mind and a good sense of what you are and aren't willing to accept. There will always be other clients.

If you've done your work in the business development process, you have allies in the organization. You have convinced someone with some amount of authority that your work is indispensable to their success. That is influence and leverage. You might hear, "That's just our policy with outside vendors," but, as with the Geneva Convention, you'll find that there is frequently more wiggle room in policy than you've been led to expect.

Contract negotiations expose misunderstandings

Some of the essential terms—like the estimated price and key deliverables—get fleshed out as you negotiate the statement of work with your client. However, a lot of gray areas may appear during this process.

For example, what does "payment due upon completion" really mean? What is "completion"? Things get ugly at the end when everyone involved doesn't have a clear shared idea of what constitutes "done." Does it mean that the website is live? Or when you deliver Photoshop files of the final design? When the client is subjectively satisfied with your work? Does the client need to send you written approval?

Settle the terms of the relationship first and save the arguments for the design.

WHAT MAKES A GOOD CONTRACT?

First off, it's good to have a contract separate from a statement of work. A contract defines the relationship between two or more parties. A statement of work defines a specific project, while a contract can cover a multitude of statements of work. For example, if you've done multiple projects with the same company you can choose to have the same contract cover all of those projects, but each project needs to have its own statement of work.

Approach contract negotiation in the spirit of fairness while being aware of the balance of power. Who is fundamentally in the pole position? It's generally going to be the client. So if you have a good handle on what their anxieties are, you can address them without gutting essential protections.

If you are dealing with a large organization that has enough lawyers sitting around to sue you out of existence in their free time, you need to stick to your guns.

Make sure your contract includes all of the following:

Intellectual property (IP) transfers on full payment

This simple little idea protects you from doing the work and getting shafted. Basically, it means that even though the work may be sitting on your clients' server, until they've paid you for it, it belongs to you. Most clients are eager to get the IP to their work, because until they do, you can make a claim on money they make through that work. Also, you can request it back.

Termination fee (or kill fee)

A termination fee protects you from walking away empty-handed should a client kill the job for reasons that are out of your control. The kill fee should cover the resources you've allotted to this particular client and the fact that you're not out looking for work because you've committed your time to this project. Lots of clients will balk at a kill fee because they think it means that you can walk out on a contract, and still make them pay. Not true. A fair contract is binding on *both* sides. Neither party can walk away without just cause.

If the client is uncomfortable with the kill fee, then don't allow them to terminate for any reason other than your material breach of the contract terms.

As a basic rule of thumb: any contract that either party can just walk away from is *not* a contract.

Deliverables acceptance language

This goes a long way toward making clients more comfortable with the provisions in your favor, such as the kill fee. The contract should state that if the client is not happy with your work they need to let you know and give you a chance to address the problem, but ultimately they can, for all intents and purposes, fire you. That means you keep the work though. Do not get fired *and* deliver the work. It sucked, remember? Should a client tell you the work is no good *and* demand the rights to it, they're probably trying to use it without paying you. This work is terrible! And the portions are so small!

Make sure your contract does not include:

Unreasonable indemnity language

This protects the client from using you as a human shield. For example: say you make some recommendations that accidentally violate a law. Stupid of you, yes, and it's something you should fix. Ultimately the client could decide to sue you instead. But indemnity means that if the client got sued they could hold you responsible for their losses. An individual or a small studio simply can't afford the insurance necessary to cover that kind of indemnity language, so avoid it.

Warranties

While you certainly design for success, and test accordingly, you simply cannot guarantee that a design will meet goals. It's like asking a college to guarantee that getting a degree from them will get you a good job. A client once asked me for a guarantee and I told him I'd give him one if we could add a bonus clause to the contract should the goals be met. That was the end of that conversation.

WHAT A CONTRACT DOESN'T DO

A contract doesn't keep things from going wrong. It merely addresses what should happen when they do. Most importantly, a contract can't make the project go right. There is no substitute for a solid client relationship coupled with good quality work—those are what make projects go well. And while a contract is essential to every project you take on, beware of the false security that might come from statements like "Don't worry. We have a contract!"

A contract will not turn the wrong client into the right client. A contract is not a parking lot for red flags. If your gut is telling you that a relationship isn't going to work out, trust your gut. It's better to be wrong by passing up a job you should have taken than to be wrong by taking a job you shouldn't have. There will always be other jobs.

ENFORCING THE CONTRACT

Once both parties have agreed to terms, signed the contract, and exchanged copies, put it away. It's there should you need it, but don't use it as a shield during the project. There will be a million small disputes while you're working together. The vast majority of these should be handled with civil conversations, always in person when possible. Handling disputes with conversation will eventually build the client relationship. Pulling out the contract at every possible opportunity will only undermine the relationship. Save it for those moments when things have actually gotten bad. Most projects don't get *that* bad. And if they do, it's a sign that you're doing something else wrong.

However, do make sure you understand everything you've agreed to and act like it. For example, if you have agreed to get approval in writing at every milestone, do that consistently. Don't get lazy just because the project seems to be going well.

If a project gets to the point where you feel like the other party isn't meeting their end of the contract, address it as soon as possible. But approach it with a positive attitude. Assume both parties want to fix it. This will be an account-level conversation. You and the client, one on one. Never whip out the contract in front of either team. You'll have an easier time negotiating your way back to good project health in private. The goal is always to finish the project well.

Should it become clear that you've reached an impasse, then it's time to call your lawyer for advice. Never threaten your client with your lawyer or with legal action until your lawyer tells you to do so.

The more careful you are when you enter into a client relationship, the more attention you pay to details and dotted i's and crossed t's, the more likely you are to get through that project doing good, successful work, and build a lasting relationship that will lead to new work and referrals for years to come.

If a jerk like me can do this, you certainly can. I guarantee you're nicer.

In ten years of business, I have never taken a client to court. I've only ever fired clients twice, and those are none of your business. I've been fired once. In the few times it hasn't worked out, the parting has usually been civil.

Except for the time it wasn't. There's no way I could write a chapter on contracts and ignore the biggest land mine of all.

WORKING WITH FRIENDS

The design and tech communities are small. You're going to work with your friends at some point. In fact, there's nothing wrong with getting a chance to pitch on a project because you're friends with somebody on the client team. You still need to sell yourself as with any other client. Nobody should hire you just because you're buddies with Jim in marketing, but being friends with Jim might get you in the room.

And, in general, having a friend on the client team isn't a problem as long as both of you behave professionally and don't abuse the relationship.

The particular land mine I'm talking about is informal projects with friends. The sort of stuff you feel funny about asking a contract for. I'd tell you to avoid these projects, but you'll just ignore me, because, let's face it, you'd feel like a giant jerk asking your buddy to sign a contract to design a few pages or make a logo for his pet project. Until your buddy sells his pet project. Now we have tension. And as bad as it is to have tension in a client relationship, it's ten times worse when a friendship is also on the line.

If you insist on doing these projects, at the very least have a conversation about possible outcomes and detail your decisions in an email to each other. That may be a bit uncomfortable (although it certainly doesn't have to be) but it may ultimately save a friendship. And it's a lot less uncomfortable than having a screaming argument with each other at a later point.

6 STICKING TO YOUR PROCESS

A WHILE BACK we were contacted about a project. A nice one; high-profile client, good budget, realistic timeline. We wanted it. We had an initial phone call with the principals and got even more excited about it. They were smart. Asked us really good questions, we gave really good answers. They told us us they were talking to a few different agencies, which never scares us. All-around good first impression.

A few days later the client told us they were asking the candidates to sketch some concepts for the proposed site to help them make their decision. And get this! They even offered to pay for it. Not bad, right?

We said no.

We told them that in order to design the right site we'd have to do our research. We'd have to talk to them about their goals, their content, their brand, how they made their money—all that stuff. And we'd have to talk to their intended audience. We'd have to take a look at the competition. Technical constraints, editorial process, content strategy, etc., etc. We needed to understand and define the problem we were being asked to solve. Then, and only then, would we propose a solution.

We told them that our process was why our work succeeded enough times that they'd heard of us. Sure, our sites are pretty, but more importantly, they work pretty well. They meet goals. And hopefully people enjoy using them as they work toward their goals, be it a customer's goal of completing a task, or the site owner's goal of getting you to register.

We told them that if we were just to do some quick sketches, without the benefit of discussion and research, the ideas would inevitably be wrong. We'd never be able to guess what was in the clients' heads. And we wouldn't put ourselves in a position where we'd be judged on our mind-reading prowess.

And as I'm telling them all this, I'm kissing the job goodbye. Which sucks, because it was a really good job, and I really wanted to do it. But the only way I could do it was if they understood and respected our process. And if you think it took guts to tell someone this, then I wish I'd had them that day, because I was totally freaked out and scared. But you have to do the right thing because it's the right thing, scared or not.

"That all makes a lot of sense. You're hired."

Thunk.

And the next time I had that same conversation with a client it was just a little less scary.

Your process is what enables you to do good work. You'll develop and tweak it throughout your entire career. Sometimes because you've learned something new, sometimes because the industry evolves and you need to reflect as much. But it will be the framework you will use to do your work.

As we tell potential clients when they ask us what their site will look like: "Oh, we have no damn idea. But we know what the process is for finding out."

WHY YOU NEED TO STICK TO YOUR PROCESS

People get to where they are in life by following a process, whether they're conscious of it or not. Successful people, like you, will be conscious of it. You'll also look for opportunities to improve it. Mind you, waking up every morning, going to a job you hate, and crying in a bathroom stall before lunch is also a process. But much like the best umbrella is the umbrella you have on you, the best process is always the one you're having success with. Don't fall for trendy processes. If the one you're using works for you, go with it.

Your successful process has also led you to enough good work that people want to keep hiring you to do more work. So, why is it that the first thing a client does upon hiring you is attempt to break the process that got them to hire you in the first place? We'll get to that in a second, but first let's discuss why you're not going to let them anymore.

I started this chapter with a story about a client who attempted to break our process. Which would have resulted in the exact opposite of what they were trying to achieve. Their goal was to ensure that they got good work. And they came up with a plan they felt did that. It's important to separate their goal from their plan because clients' goals are generally worthwhile. At least clients you've allowed to get this far into the conversation. Their plans, however, are a whole other matter.

Planning how to achieve a goal needs to be something you take charge of. That's *your* job. And unless you show the client that you are taking charge of that you're going to have a very hard time getting anything done during the project.

In this particular case, I addressed the client's goal by ensuring that they'd get good work because we had a process for getting good work done. I addressed their actual concern. And presented my own plan. And they were open-minded enough to listen to it, and I managed to convince them their goals would be better met with my plan than theirs. Just as importantly, I followed up by achieving that goal.

Now should a client immediately step off the minute you announce you have a process? I'd be surprised if they did. You need to sell. When a client hires you they are hiring your process as well, but you need to sell them on that process as the reason you do good work. And that needs to be done as part of the hiring process, not after.

"If we're going to work together, here's how it's going to work."

You're not going to ask for permission to do things your way. You're going to convince clients that your way works by showing them how you will use your process to meet their goals. And you'll back this up by showing them how many times it's worked in the past. And every time you manage to do this you'll have yet one more example to make your case. Making the next time you have to do this that much less scary.

Our process works. So will yours. If you stick to it. And fight for it.

WHY COMPANIES ATTEMPT TO BREAK YOUR PROCESS

Companies love talking a studio out of the process that got them to hire them. Which is akin to signing Roy Halladay and then asking him to play the outfield. (Yes, it's a baseball metaphor—I'll walk you through it.) Roy Halladay is possibly the greatest pitcher of his generation. He'd be a terrible outfielder. But imagine some VP in the organization decided that since they'd just sunk a lot of money into signing him, they'd better get the most use out of him. So they should put him at a position that plays every day, instead of having him pitch. (Starting pitchers go once every five days.) In this metaphor baseball is standing in for design and the stupid VP is still the stupid VP.

So why would someone do this? Anxiety. Anxiety about having spent the money. Anxiety about needing to see what they perceive as "results" as soon as possible. Anxiety at having made the wrong decision. And ultimately, anxiety about their own job security should they have made the wrong decision in hiring you.

When people get anxious they fall back into the terrible habits that make up their comfort places. And, by definition, problem solving and innovation don't happen in our comfort places.

Throughout a project you may have to remind a client multiple times that they agreed to follow your process. And throughout a project you will have to convince a client that your process is actually on target to get them the results they need.

There will be hand-holding. There will be tough love. But above all, you will have to stand your ground and stick to what you know works. You will also need to be flexible enough to alleviate a client's anxiety without putting the project in jeopardy. A good process, like a building built on a fault line (like the one I'm writing in right now!) is built to give enough so that it doesn't break.

HOW COMPANIES ATTEMPT TO BREAK YOUR PROCESS

A short selection of popular favorites.

Start drawing (solving) before you fully understand the problem

This is a no. The anxiety here comes from a basic misunderstanding that they hired you to design and design is pictures. They're not sure why you're doing this other stuff. And if you've ever walked into a visual presentation and said, "Today we're finally going to look at design!" you're part of the reason this problem exists, so stop blaming your clients. You need to start every project with an explanation of what designing something looks like. And how all the pieces fit together. And the minute you start putting "pictures" in front of people, you're going to have to address their reactions to those pictures. Don't put yourself in a position where you have to defend either your own work or their reaction to it before you have the research to know whether it's right or wrong.

Work out of order

You know what the least important page of a website is? The home page. More likely than not it's a one-off template, it doesn't expose enough of the navigational system, and quite often it's more controlled by the needs of marketing than the site's users. Yet this is the page clients want to see the most. I often describe it as building the roof of the house first and then letting it sit until we go back and build the walls.

I hate starting with the home page. However, I've found that until clients see it we can't get their attention on anything else. So, we give them a home page. And while they debate its merits we get cranking on the rest of the site. We bend, but we don't break.

Try to do your work for you

The most common instance of this, by far, is "We've already done a lot of research. So we can just hand it to you and skip that whole phase." And yes, seeing that research will be helpful, but it doesn't take the place of us having to do our own. The point isn't to do research—it's to understand. It's not a checklist item that we're happy to allow someone else to cross off.

The second most common instance is clients developing competing visuals. That's a deal breaker. Never put yourself in a situation where you're competing to solve a problem you've been entrusted to solve. Plus, you need the room to try things that may or may not be right without the calvary being called in.

I love competing to get work, but once I get it, it's mine. The competition is over.

Control or block your access to people

Welcome to the world of internal dysfunction. Bob is your client and Bob is in a power struggle with Mary, but you need to get information from Mary to do the job, but Bob doesn't want you to talk to Mary because he's afraid he'll look weak, or he doesn't want Mary to know what's going on. There's no way this ends well. Have a talk with Bob before the project starts. Make sure he knows that you will need direct access to people to do the project. If he hesitates, figure out what the problem is; perhaps Bob just wants to make sure he's in the room when you talk to certain people.

But if Bob isn't willing to give you access to other people in the company, that's usually a sign of a bigger problem. Like perhaps the project isn't really that important to the company, or he doesn't have the support he needs to carry the project to fruition.

Rush

I love having a sense of urgency around a project. But certain things will take the time they will take. The popular saying is that you can't throw nine women at a baby and get it in a month. (I have tried this, and it is true!) Rushing leads to stupid mistakes, like launching a site filled with lorem ipsum (not that anyone's ever done that of course). What's worth doing is worth doing well, and even while working in an urgent manner, details must be looked after and quality needs to stay at a high level.

And I guarantee you that the client who wants to rush the most is the same one that spent a month or more waffling to sign the job.

Waffle over decisions

Nothing derails a project faster than waffling over decisions, whether it's taking too long to make a decision, or revisiting decisions that have already been acted on. You either have a team sitting on their hands waiting, or a team working backward to unravel what they've made.

You can protect yourself against this by making sure your client understands the repercussions of waffling. Everything on a project has a cost associated with it. Be it time or money or both. Clients hate wasting time and money, and in many cases don't have the resources or authority to get more of either. So when asking them to make a decision, make sure to also tell them the cost associated with it.

"If we get an answer to this by Wednesday, then we can move forward and meet the Friday deadline. But anything beyond a decision by 6 p.m. will push us to Monday, and move all the subsequent deadlines out as well. Which means we'll need budget for an extra four days of work."

Obviously, you want to tailor that statement to the situation. Don't pull out a battle ax when a reassuring tap on the shoulder is enough. Just make sure your client understands that there's no magic trick that allows for 120 hours of work on the last week of the project.

You can do a lot to show a client how valuable time is in how you comport yourself throughout the project. Run your meetings and work sessions efficiently. Come in prepared. Don't run over. Don't hang out. Don't train clients to think you've got extra time on your hands. As far as they're concerned, you scoped twelve weeks for this project, there was one right before it, and there's another one right after it.

Waffling endangers that valuable precious resource.

Ignore project goals in favor of organizational politics

"Because the CEO said so." Every project is subject to one or two peccadilloes from a higher up that make absolutely no sense to anyone. This is a matter of picking your battles. Some of their requests will have absolutely no affect on the overall experience or success of the site. Some of them can be devastating. One CEO demanded that the site contain a photo of a particular local landmark so users knew where they were located. This was of utmost importance to him, and relatively easy to accommodate. (It's on his bio page, by the way.)

A lot of organizational politics are a consequence of people not feeling heard. This is why you should aim to include as may people as possible in kickoff meetings. Even if they're ultimately not part of the project team, give them an opportunity to be heard. You'll find out useful information that your main contact might have assumed you didn't need to know. You can also learn a lot from who your contact attempts to omit from such meetings.

Ultimately your client may ask you to do something on the project that's detrimental to the project's goal because they've been told to do it, and they're understandably unwilling to defy a higher up's request. You need to be willing to take that bullet. After all, you don't have to work with these people beyond the project. You can push them a little harder. And you need to be willing to have difficult conversations within the organization that your main client may be unwilling or unable to have.

Try a new trendy way of doing things

As a designer it's your job to differentiate between innovation and a trend. And to get your client to strive for the former while ignoring the latter. You can usually do this by pointing them to the last big trend that's just started backfiring and enjoying a moment of awkward laughter together.

And please, let's all stop with those ridiculous wrap-around banners. Enough already.

HOW YOU CAN ASSURE YOUR CLIENT THINGS ARE GOING WELL

At the risk of sounding like a broken record (ask your parents), stay in good communication with your clients at all times. They will accept your process as long as you are showing them results. Make sure to set their expectations correctly as to what is happening when. And once they happen let them know you're on track.

Should they get off track make sure to communicate that as well. How you handle the communication of something going badly and how quickly you can implement a plan for getting back on track is ultimately more important than going off track to begin with.

A good client will trust your process as long as they have transparency into it, can see results, and you're willing to bend a little here and there. Without breaking.

7
PRESENTING DESIGN

A DESIGNER WHO does not present his or her own work is not a designer. Presenting the work, explaining the rationale, answering questions, and eliciting feedback are part of the design toolkit. If you sit at your desk while someone else presents work to the client, you don't get to complain about the feedback. The failure was yours.

I've been presenting design to clients and internal teams for a long time (Bush, Sr., was in the White House when I started), and I still get anxious about it. It may have been a while since I've thrown up in a client's bathroom and washed off next to the person I'd eventually be presenting to, sure, but I still get nerves.

The fact that I'm sitting here telling you how to present design isn't a testament that I was born with some great skill—it's a testament that anyone can present design if they're willing to pick themselves up off the floor and just keep at it.

There is no substitute for learning how to present design other than presenting design. Be nervous. No one ever died from a poor presentation. At some point you'll realize that your nerves are lying to you. The evidence that you *can* present design will grow too large to ignore. You'll do it again and again, and one day you'll realize that you're not as terrified as you used to be. Stay there. You're actually designing from that point forward.

IT'S NOT GOING TO SELL ITSELF

The biggest myth ever perpetuated in the design field is that good design sells itself. (The second is that Copperplate is a legitimate typeface.) Design can't speak for itself any more than a tamale can take off its own husk. You're presenting a solution to a business problem, and you're presenting it as an advocate for the end users. The client needs to know that you've studied the problem, understood its complexities, and that you're working from that understanding.

Stop trying to get your clients to "understand design" and instead show them that you understand what they hired you to do. Explain how the choices you've made lead to a successful project. This isn't magic, it's math. Show your work. Don't *hope* someone "gets it," and don't blame them if they don't—convince them.

If you're confident enough that you're putting the right solution in front of a client, which you better be, you need to pass that confidence along to the client. Ultimately, your job is to make the client feel confident in the design. Confidence is as much of a deliverable as anything you're handing over in the project.

WHY YOU NEED TO PRESENT YOUR OWN WORK

It bears repeating.

Being able to present your own work is a core design skill. It helps build rapport with the client. It puts the person directly responsible for the work in front of them. It shows them that you're presenting that work with confidence. And it gives them an opportunity to ask questions directly of the person who did the work.

When I was a kid we played a game called telephone. All the kids form a circle, and the lead kid whispers a word in the ear of the kid next to them. That kid whispers the word to the kid next to him, and so on, until the word gets whispered in *your* ear. (Shut up. The Xbox hadn't been invented yet.) Without fail, the word that got whispered in your ear was different than the word you started with. "Chocolate" would become "chick lit," "baseball" would become "base board," and "let's go to church" would become "let's go smoke in the alley." You get the idea.

When clients are speaking to you through an intermediary you're not hearing directly from them. You can't see their face. That's important. Quite often the look on their face will tell you much more than the words out of their mouth.

Things that were posed as questions, such as, "Why is the logo that size?" get reported back to you as statements like, "Make the logo bigger." You weren't there to answer the question. In fact, you didn't even know it was posed as a question.

As a designer, you need to become adept at interpreting what a client actually means. You need to be there to ask clarifying questions. You need to manage the presentation process as carefully as you make the work.

This also applies to work that's not being presented in person. If you're working with a long-distance client, set up a phone call so that you can present the work and the rationale. And don't send the work in advance. Reveal it during the call, after you've had the opportunity to set the stage properly. The last thing you want is clients getting ahead of you and starting a call with their list of proposed changes before you've had a chance to present.

If you're working at an agency that won't let you present your own work, make the case for how it benefits everyone. It helps you, it helps the client, it helps the project get done correctly. If they still won't let you present your own work, get the hell out. They're not letting you do your job. Don't work at a place that doesn't let you do your job correctly.

HAVE AN AGENDA

Before you ever get in a room with a client, let them know *why* you're getting in that room. (If *you're* not sure why you're meeting, then maybe there's no reason to meet.) Make sure everyone is walking in with the same expectations and knows what's expected of them. Also, let them know how long the presentation is scheduled for, and give them the desired outcome.

A meeting without an agenda is an invitation for everyone to bring their pet issues. After all, you can't really stray off course if no course has been set.

BE CONFIDENT IN WHAT YOU'RE SHOWING

There should be absolutely no doubt that this is your meeting. Stand up. Walk to the head of the room. Announce who you are, what you do, reiterate the goals of the project and tell people how what you're about to show them will meet those goals.

Put your audience at ease by letting them know that they're exactly the right people to have in the room, and what you need from them is their expertise with the product or service, not design knowledge.

Steer the discussion away from personal subjectivity by outlining good topics of feedback: how well the proposed solutions meet specific metrics, whether their voice and brand are coming through, etc. Encourage them to stay in their own zone of expertise and they won't attempt to hop on yours.

Never apologize for what you're *not* showing. By the time you're presenting, you should be focused on presenting what you have, not making excuses for what you don't. And you need to believe what you're saying to convince the client of the same. If you think the work is on the way to meeting their goals then say *that*. Design is an iterative process, done with a client's proper involvement at key points. The goal isn't always to present finished work; it's to present work at the right time.

I've met a few designers over the years who feel like selling design is manipulation. Manipulation is convincing someone that the truth is different than what it seems. You're familiar with the marketing phrase, "Sell the sizzle, not the steak?" Well, if the steak sucks, that's manipulation. If the steak backs up the sizzle's promise then it's good salesmanship. If you believe the work is good, and you can stand before a client and make an honest attempt at convincing them of the same by using the research you've done, then what you are doing is selling good design.

Don't be arrogant. Confidence means you believe you'll succeed because you've done the research, you understand the problem, and the work you're presenting backs that up. Arrogance is believing you'll succeed despite not having done those things. Don't be that jerk.

SPEAK TO GOALS, NOT FEATURES

Your review of the work should be goal-driven. And prioritized. The client had major goals with this project. They'll be anxious to see how those goals are addressed. Go there first, and do it in a way that maps to their goal and not to your manifestation of the goal. For example:

"Here's a Twitter button!" is bad.

"As you can see, we've addressed your social media concerns!" is better.

"We've placed social media sharing tools in places alongside the article where testing shows the reader is most likely to interact with them, and designed that space so that it's flexible enough to add and subtract services as they rise and fall from prominence," is the best of all.

Remember that every feature is there for a reason. Lead with the reason. And if you don't have a good reason why it's there, that's probably a sign it's not needed.

DON'T GIVE A REAL ESTATE TOUR

The most obvious sign that a designer is nervous is the real estate tour. You've seen this. The presenter will start at the top left of the page, telling you where the logo is, describing how it "pops," then move right and down, describing every element along the way, taking you on a guided tour of every element on the page, winding up at the copyright notice in the footer. They'll make no mention of goals or benefits. In the process they'll leave themselves totally open to clients pulling up with construction teams and cranes to do some remodeling.

Don't waste a client's time walking them through what they can already see. Your job is to explain how what they're looking at is the best way to achieve their goals.

If you start with the declaration that you're accommodating the social media strategy, there's a lot less resistance because you'll be showing that every visual element is in a particular place for a reason. Otherwise it just sounds like you're dropping buttons in random spots.

GIVE THE CLIENT PERMISSION TO GO NEGATIVE

It can be incredibly difficult for clients to say anything negative about your work. Something about "upsetting the sensitive, talented creatives." Or just basic, if misguided, decency. This doesn't help the project. Unspoken expectations lead to seething unspoken frustration, which ultimately bursts forth in a gruesome mess when you've run out of budget.

Let them know that negative feedback is an essential part of the process and a part of the client's job. We prefer constructive and well-reasoned negative feedback, but even an outburst of "Never show me that crap again!" saves everyone a lot of time.

At the beginning of every visual design presentation, particularly in the early stages, we give a little speech, some variation of, "Today, we are going to show you some things that may not be right. If you see something that isn't working, you need to point it out. If you don't tell us what you think isn't working, we will show you the same thing again and again until we are out of time and money and you are stuck with it."

We've found this exercise makes everyone a lot more comfortable with the process and saves a lot of time wasted by clients saying, "Yeah, that seems fine" when they're thinking, "That is a pile of noxious crap for our customers to poop on. I hope they can read my mind so I don't have to say it."

HELP YOUR CLIENT GIVE YOU THE INFORMATION YOU NEED

More often than not the designers who complain that clients give them subjective feedback are the ones most prone to asking for subjective feedback. Everyone gets the feedback they deserve.

Stay away from questions like "Do you like it?" You weren't hired to make something they liked. Ask your clients to comment specifically about the things you want them to address. Avoid talking about things you don't want them to go into. "What do you guys think of the size of the logo?" for example.

They will, of course, still give you feedback about things you may not want feedback about. Most of it you just need to hear and acknowledge. But if they're persistent, ask them to map what they are asking for to a goal, and follow up with clarifying questions. Oftentimes a client's prescriptive feedback needs to be unpacked to get to the real issue.

WHEN PRESENTING WITH A TEAM

If you're presenting with a team, you and everyone else has a role to play. Your job is to take the responsibility for selling the design work. But you may not be the only designer on the project. If you've been working collaboratively, present collaboratively. Just make sure that you've clearly outlined who's taking charge where.

You may also have a project manager on your side who does the initial project recap. They should also keep track of time management and the agenda.

And while everyone should have a set role, be flexible enough to let everyone play to their strengths. If your interaction designer has been championing the faceted navigation model you're proposing, let her pitch it. Weave other people into the presentation as seamlessly as possible.

Cover your teammates' backs during the presentation. If they're looking lost or confused, jump in, finish their sentence, and let them jump back in when they recover. Don't throw to another member of the team when they aren't expecting it ("...and now Jason will explain our take on the advertising model to you...").

Always present with a united front. No matter how much arguing there might have been back at the office, by the time you're in front of a client, every solution you're presenting is a team solution. Should a client propose something similar to what had been shot down internally earlier in the week, anyone who screams, "That's what *I* wanted!" gets punched in the neck then and there.

Of course I'm kidding. No punching until you're back in the office.

BE OPEN TO BEING WRONG

Confidence also means you can handle being wrong. And you will be. Many times. The goal of a presentation isn't to shove your decisions down a client's throat—it's to present what you believe to be right in a manner that also persuades others that it's right. And it also means allowing them to convince you that you're wrong. I can't tell you how many times I've walked into a presentation totally confident that what I was presenting was rock solid, only to have a client come up with an obvious use case that I'd overlooked and which brought the whole thing to a crashing halt. And that's good. Because part of the design process is finding those holes. Be glad you're working with a smart client. Don't keep trying to sell something that's broken. Acknowledge you were wrong, and be thankful for the new insight.

NEVER EMBARRASS YOUR CLIENT

Chances are your main client contact reports to someone. Someone who may be meeting you for the first time during this presentation. (Make sure you know this in advance!) Whether this is the CEO, or one of thirty-two "Executive" VPs, not only is your work under scrutiny, but so is your client's judgment in hiring you. Do them a favor and make them look good. Be prepared. Be honest. Engage them in the conversation and listen to their feedback. This person is your ally, and helping his stock rise within the organization can only help you in this project and future ones.

END STRONG

End on time. Respect your client's time and show them that yours is valuable as well.

Make sure everyone's questions have been answered. And make sure they have an avenue for feedback, which we'll discuss in the next chapter, as well as a deadline. Thank them for their time. Shake hands and offer to take your glass to the sink. They'll tell you to leave it, but offer anyway. Your mother raised you well.

Which reminds me of a fabulous story from the pre-Mule days. I was working with another studio and we'd just gone through a particularly difficult presentation. Couldn't wait to get out of the client's office. We said our goodbyes, packed up our stuff, and headed to the elevator. While we're waiting for the elevator our creative director turns to me and says, "God, she was a bitch!" just as said bitch came walking around the corner.

The rest of the project was awkward.

My advice to you when you finish the presentation is to thank everyone for their time. Shut your mouth. Pack up your laptop. Head out of the building. Walk out the front door. Around the corner. In the car. Across the bridge. Okay, *now* you can talk.

Or, just make it a habit never to speak ill of your clients. They're paying your bills. And putting their livelihood in your hands. They're good people.

8 MANAGING FEEDBACK

GATHERING AND MANAGING FEEDBACK is an essential part of the design process. And next to Adobe updater updates, it's the thing designers complain about the most. Complaints range from "They're not telling me what to do!" to "They're telling me what to do!" to "Oh, God! They sent a PowerPoint comp!"

We're far enough along in this book now that I bet you can guess what's coming. That's right: I love you, but it's *your* fault. You can't assume clients will know how to give you the right feedback at the right time and in the right manner. What you *can* assume, however, is that both you and the client are trying to get to the same goal: a successful project. So take a deep breath. And let's figure out how to get what you need.

SETTING THE STAGE FOR GOOD FEEDBACK

No matter how smart or articulate a person is, no one intuitively knows how to give useful design feedback. This skill is not part of anyone's day job (except for art directors). How to give feedback must be taught. And the teaching starts at the very beginning of the project. When you decide to take on a client, and explain your process to them, make sure you explain how their feedback is crucial to making the process work. Both of you have a role to play and the feedback is the rich sinewy connective tissue between both parties.

Has your client bought design services before? How often, how long ago? And what role did he or she play? Get a proper gauge of your clients' experience with design feedback. And realize that "A lot!" may not be a good answer. Experience working with freelancers may not translate well to working with a large design consultancy, and vice versa. And neither translates to working with a small shop. In the end, you will have to both show your client how to work with you and, more importantly, you'll have to learn how to work with your client.

Work with your client to establish a feedback cycle that works for both of you. At Mule, we generally like getting feedback no more than forty-eight hours after a presentation so we don't lose momentum. Some companies have too many stakeholders to make this possible, so neither should you require it, nor should they agree to it in that case. You'd both be setting yourselves up to fail. Come to a good compromise. But make sure they understand that more time for feedback means the project completion date moves back as well.

Some companies move faster, and want to promise you feedback in twenty-four hours. That's great! Give them forty-eight. Companies that move faster also have to put out a lot more fires, and generally with a smaller staff. Probably the people who are supposed to be giving you their feedback are manning the hose.

Either way, document the agreed-upon feedback cycle in writing and put it in the Statement of Work. It's a deadline, subject to the typical accolades that come from meeting a deadline and remonstrations that come with missing one.

THE INVISIBLE STAKEHOLDER

This is also when those invisible stakeholders you didn't do a good enough job of ferreting out make their presence felt. We've all met these lovely people. They show up during the third week of development with thoughts about the design concept. Or the team you've been working with for three months will announce that once the site is ready to "launch" they'll unveil it to the board to get their thoughts. You will feel tricked when this happens. You know how you should really be feeling? That's right—dumb. Because you didn't flush them out early in the process.

Going into a project, you need to know who on the client side provides input, who gives feedback, and who approves. You may have a better idea of who these people should be than your client. As you meet people within the organization during the discovery phase (because you have one, right?) ask yourself whether they're someone who can insert themselves into the feedback cycle later. Be proactive and have a discussion with your main contact about involving them sooner rather than later. If they decide they won't be participating in reviews, then you'll have to hold them to that later. As important as it is to have a small feedback group reviewing design decisions, it's even more important that it's the *right* group.

The general rule is to involve as many people as possible in early discussions, and make that number as small as possible once you go into review cycles. Often, people on the client side say they want to remain involved, but really just want to tell you the one thing they care about and then get back to their day job. If they don't get to tell you that one thing, then they will pop up at the end of the project all bent out of shape.

YOUR CLIENT IS NOT AN EXPERT IN GIVING FEEDBACK

There's nothing less helpful to the client than telling them you want open-ended "feedback." Your clients need your help in figuring out what kind of feedback you're looking for. They need structure and guidance. And if you provide that structure and guidance ahead of time there's a far greater chance that you'll be getting the kind of structured feedback you'll need to move forward, and save everyone a lot of time.

Most clients tend to feel self-conscious about voicing their opinion about design. How often have you heard, "I don't know anything about design!" That's fine; they don't have to. What they do know something about, however, is their business, and what you're actually looking for here is business feedback. You need to know whether the design work is meeting the business goals of the project. You say "design," and clients hear "art," and now everyone's uncomfortable. Act like the design expert the client hired; remind them—if need be—that they hired a design expert, and their job is to be the business experts. Keep them in their comfort zone and they're less likely to come back with feedback from a family member who's got "a good sense of design."

Of course our dirty little secret is that while we're telling our clients to be objective, and to keep personal preferences out of it, there's nothing we want more than them to like it. The first step in getting objective feedback is to make sure we're giving objective presentations and keeping our own feelings out of the mix.

FEEDBACK GUIDELINES

We prepare feedback guidelines for the client before presentations. We tell them what's helpful to talk about and what's not. They're thankful for the guidance and it saves them a lot of time. Clients love it when you save them time. We tell them what decisions are relevant at this point, what to ignore, and what may require further clarification. We also reiterate key points made during the presentation so they don't forget.

For example, let's say we just did our first visual concept presentation for a website. If we did it right, then the comps we showed were loose and sketchy and focused on tone, not specific functionality. And they were probably done before site architecture was finalized. The last thing we want is a lot of feedback about missing functionality. So the feedback guidelines might say:

Focus on:

- Overall tone (Does this site *feel* like your company?)
- Voice (Is it using language the right way? Is it friendly? Authoritative? Trustworthy?)
- Structure (Too dense? Not dense enough?)

Ignore:

- Specific labels and body copy (Why is everything in Latin?)
- Missing elements (Where's my newsletter signup?)
- Things we did not show you (I have comments about the company history page.)

It's also a good idea to address personal preferences before any feedback is given, rather than after, at which point you risk making people feel dumb for liking green, which although not the right color for this project, is a very lovely color in and of itself. Unlike mauve.

Feedback guidelines should be short enough to be helpful, and not long enough to be considered additional work. Go over them with the client during the presentation and make yourself available should they require more clarification. Make sure every member of the team gets them so they're all playing under the same rules.

And know that they'll give you feedback on everything you asked them to ignore anyway. Clients will gravitate toward what they're worried about the most, or what they're most comfortable with. Feel free to ignore it until the time is right.

THE MOST IMPORTANT FEEDBACK GUIDELINE OF ALL

Many clients believe that proper feedback means telling a designer how to fix something, or what is known as prescriptive feedback. Many designers complain about prescriptive feedback, unless they don't get it. At which point they complain they don't know what the client wants. Yes, our reputation as being difficult is well-deserved.

Let's remember that clients aren't experts in giving design feedback and—I'm gonna go out on a limb here—venture that most of the time they're the problem solver on their teams. Let them know that not only are these *your* problems to solve, but that they're paying you to solve them.

You need to start holding this line during presentations, as clients jump in with suggestions on things they're not happy about. Impromptu prescriptive work sessions during presentations can eat up a lot of time, and put you in the awkward spot of having to tell clients that their suggestions may not be very good. So let them know ahead of time, "If something isn't working, tell us why and we'll fix it. We want to earn our money." Remind them again in the written guidelines.

You don't want to put yourself in a position of carrying out your client's design decisions. If you allow them to start designing for you, you have no one to blame but yourself. If they insist on prescriptive feedback it's time for an account-level conversation. Anyone who hires you because they thought you could do the job and then doesn't let you do it has lost respect for either you or the design process.

Can you put "no prescriptive feedback" in the contract? I suppose you could, if you really wanted to. But ultimately I think this is one of those times you just need to be able to work without a net. Keep the contract to legal issues, and use your design skills and backbone to support your design process.

GETTING FEEDBACK ON TIME

As I mention above, set up a deadline for turning feedback around. Any time you're requesting feedback, remind the client how much time they have and get them to commit to meeting the deadline. (The success of every project is the hundreds of little commitments made along the way.) Let them know that if something comes up that might put the deadline in jeopardy, they should let you know right away. That goes for both parties. The minute a deadline is in jeopardy notify the other party. There are many reasons for missing a deadline, but there is only one for not notifying the other party. (That's a free life tip, kids.)

The longer clients are taking to get you feedback, the more likely that they're not just pointing out issues, but working out solutions. You, or your project manager, need to get them on the phone. Ask them if they need your team's help with anything. Remind them to come back with questions, and not solutions. That usually goes a little something like this:

"What's up with our feedback, Bob?"

"We're not happy with global nav, but we're not sure how to fix it."

"Well, just tell us why you're not happy with it. We'll come up with something. That's why you're paying us, Bob."

"That'd be swell. Cause we're stumped."

Most clients try to fix things because they believe it's the right thing to do. And unless you tell them it's not you have no one to blame but yourself.

HOW TO READ CLIENT FEEDBACK

Eventually the blessed day will come when the client sends you his feedback. Oh, did I tell you to get it in writing? You need to get it in writing. An email is just fine. Immediately acknowledge getting it, thank them for sending it. And sit back. Relax. It's important that you're relaxed when reading client feedback. Open your mind to the possibilities that you might be going on a journey. Client feedback has a way of taking you to places you never dreamed you'd go. But, honestly, remember two very important things:

- You're both working toward the same goal with the best of intentions.
- Most clients haven't been trained in how to give feedback. (Well, except by you.)

First off, do yourself a favor and just read the whole thing straight through at least once. Resist the urge to read it aloud to the rest of your team, if you have one, because mocking a client's feedback reflects poorly on you. They're gonna say some weird stuff. They're honestly trying. Give them a break. Don't share the feedback with anyone else until you're sure you can do it in a calm, reassuring manner. (Pro tip: sometimes my partner Erika withholds feedback from me for days. We're totally in a "do as I say, not as I do" zone here.)

Your job is now to take the client's feedback and put it into an actionable form.

ORGANIZING FEEDBACK

Your first job is to separate the actionable feedback from the non-actionable feedback. Sometimes clients just like to document their thought process. Your job is to sift through and find the actionable from the non-actionable.

"At first I thought this work reminded me of something I didn't like, but then it didn't and then it did again and then the reason I thought it did was because the typeface was similar, but then I changed my mind again and realized it was because it was blue."

There is absolutely nothing you can do. Let it go.

On the other hand, "We've changed our strategy!" is not feedback. Nor is anything that even hints at it. It's a shift in goals to be addressed immediately at the account level.

Having separated the feedback from the non-feedback, it's time to make three lists.

To-do

No brainers. Stuff you can change immediately.

Disagreements

Things that run counter to the goals of the project, disrupt the design, break conventions, or don't jive with the client's brand. Or, they're just bad ideas. Don't do bad design! Prepare to make your case to the client about every issue on this list. You're going to have to convince them. It's usually not as hard as you think. Clients listen to reason more than you give them credit for. You're just going to have to persuade them. Part of the job.

Clarification needed

If you don't understand something on the client's feedback list, pick up the phone and ask them about it. Don't try to read their minds. Once you've gotten clarification on this list, move to one of the other two lists.

If you have a team now is a good time to go over the list with them. You'll be organized and relaxed, and seeing that you've called out issues to discuss further with the client will probably keep your team relaxed as well.

Let's get on the phone.

GOING OVER FEEDBACK WITH YOUR CLIENT

Have we talked about how awesome talking to your client in person is? Every time you deal with your client in person is an opportunity to build trust. And to remind each other of why you chose to work together. So whenever possible, meet with your client in person, *especially* if you have a long list of feedback you disagree with. When that's not possible, get them on the phone. Hear each others' voices. The last thing you want to be is another in a long list of emails. Everyone hates email.

Start by thanking your client for the feedback. Go over the no-brainer list. That's a quick win. Mention any particularly good suggestions they made. You need to build up some good-will for what's coming.

With one exception: tackle the elephant in the room immediately. If one of the items on the discussion list is big enough to derail the schedule—or undoes some previously-agreed to decisions—dive right into it. Make sure your client knows the impact this issue has in terms of time and cost.

Your strategy with all the discussion items is to present your case rationally. Tell them why you disagree, use the research you did, use data, use relevant writing on the topic. Let them know how their decision might run counter to the goals of the project. And, yes, use aesthetics. That's one of the reasons they hired you, right? Make the business case, but also make the design case. After all, you can't always talk someone out of using Copperplate for business reasons.

You won't win all the fights. But you might find yourself winning more of them each time you try. More importantly, you'll learn which ones are worth fighting for and which ones you can win. You'll also learn the fine art of horse trading. I once argued with a client for an hour over an issue I didn't care about (eventually letting him win!), because I *really* cared about the next issue coming up. At that point, he was so tired out and savoring his victory that he gave in almost immediately. Arguments are also things to be designed.

After going over feedback with your client, make sure you detail all of your decisions in writing, and have them reply with an acknowledgement so you're both on the same page as to where to go next.

WHEN CLIENTS COMP

You thought maybe I wasn't gonna address this? I just saved it for dessert.

There is nothing less helpful than getting feedback in the form of a comp (whether committed in Photoshop, PowerPoint, or Word). Nothing. I mean it. We've been in business at Mule for almost ten years now, and this is the only thing we've ever fired a client over. (It happened once. The client refused to stop after being told on numerous occasions it was counter-productive, not to mention a contract violation.)

Your best bet is to nip this in the bud before it happens. Yes, put it in the contract. Now put it in your back pocket for safe keeping. As we've discussed before, your contract is your safety net and your life support. You should be able to avoid this problem by using something from your design toolbox. Namely, your amazing skills of persuasion.

Remind your client when requesting feedback that if something isn't working for them to point it out and go into as much detail as possible as to why they feel it's not working. Ask them to tie it to the goals agreed to earlier in the project. More than anything, their *reasoning* is critical to solving the problem. Being told to just do something a certain way—or worse, getting a comp of it—only means you have to reverse-engineer the whole thing and find out what you were trying to solve. Lost time, lost budget.

They might do it anyway. *Now* can we whip out the contract and beat them with it? Not so fast; your goal is *always* to come to an amicable solution first. There's nuance at play here.

There's a difference between comping to communicate and comping to substitute.

If your client took your comp and haphazardly started chopping it up and moving things around and even adding things from other sites, they're probably just trying to communicate with you. Yes, there's a better way to do it, for sure. But these are the acts of someone trying to get a message across. You yourself are probably more comfortable showing solutions than describing them, right? That's what's going on here. It's not malice. It's still a pain in the ass, though; and it deserves a reminder that, while it may be the most comfortable way for them to get their point across, it's the least helpful way for you to receive it.

It's worth a sit down. Have them walk through the comp and explain to you why they made the changes they did. This can be used as an exercise on both sides. Either they felt like they couldn't get their point across verbally, or that you wouldn't understand it. A walk-through can solve both of those problems.

On the other hand, suppose the client delivers their feedback in the form of a totally different comp than the one you presented. "We were hoping for something more like *this*."

More often than not, this happens when there's an internal designer on the client team who's not happy about outside help being brought in. Put yourself in their shoes. You might even do the same thing. Don't. (We'll cover working with internal designers in more detail later in the book.)

My first question to you is whether you knew this designer existed already or not. If so, you needed to make an ally out of him earlier in the process. If not, you didn't do your due diligence. Either way you're in a spot.

You are now in a position where you're competing for a job you've already earned. That is unacceptable. Do not, under *any* circumstances, discuss the new comp with your client. Once you do you've validated its existence. Pull them aside. If you're working with a team, this is a job for your team leader to handle; it's account level. Remind the client that they've hired you for this job, and if they feel that you're no longer capable of fulfilling it, then a larger discussion is needed. See if the client is willing to play by the rules, as they signed up to do; if they are, great. You'll still need a strategy for dealing with that designer. I'd suggest keeping him close. If you can't come to an agreement then be ready to walk away. Never, ever, threaten to walk away from a job. You either walk away or you don't. But if you were hired to do a job and are now being asked to compete for it, then the job has changed. Your next call is to your lawyer.

LET'S END ON A HAPPY NOTE

Ninety-nine percent of your clients are good people with honest intentions. They may not give you perfect feedback every time, but their intent is good, and you share the same goal of doing kick-ass work together. As long as there's mutual respect you can get past a couple of hiccups in the process. There are always hiccups in the process.

In ten years of business at Mule, we've dealt with a lot of client comping. Only once did we terminate a project because of it. And we gave the client multiple opportunities to stop. It was a great lesson to get out of the way early. You may never have to deal with it yourself, but if you do, you'll have the tools to handle it.

9 GETTING YOUR MONEY

EVER SINCE starting our podcast, *Let's Make Mistakes,* Katie Gillum and I have received a substantial amount of email from designers looking for advice of one sort or another. Most of it is from young designers just starting out on their career path. The topics vary from client-related questions like, "Where do I get some?" to craft-based questions like, "How long should I work on a concept?"

The vast, and I mean *vast,* majority of the questions, however, are sad stories about late payments, or sadder stories about payments that are never coming. The saddest example I saw was from a designer whose client offered to settle up if the designer would do "just a little more work." I hate to see a designer not being paid for their work, almost as much as I hate seeing a designer not doing their job to ensure they get paid.

The best way to deal with late payments is to keep them from ever being late. And it takes a combination of good terms, clearly defined agreements, and, most importantly, relationship building to ensure that checks keep flowing at a good healthy pace. It's bad enough to worry about where the rent is coming from, but it's worse to have to worry about it even after earning the dough for it.

Sometimes no matter how much due diligence you do you'll still get sideswiped. Companies reorganize, companies get bought, projects get de-prioritized, and so on. None of these are things you have any control over, but with the right systems in place you can not only survive this stuff, but walk away with your check in hand.

Let me tell you a story. A few years ago our team was working on a project with a new division of a pretty large company. We'd done our due diligence. They were solid. The budget was approved in a timely fashion without much haggling, as was the contract. The team we were working with was opinionated, smart, and to this day, one of my favorite teams to have had the pleasure to work with. A few months into the project, the work was going really well. Honestly, this was one of those projects where both sides really egged each other on to do better work. So much so that they decided to expand the scope of the work, which we were thrilled about. We submitted a change order, which they had verbally agreed to, but not yet signed.

One day we go in for a work session and the place is eerily quiet. We're ushered into an empty office and told to wait for someone to come talk to us. At first I think we're getting shit-canned, but then I realize that wouldn't explain the office being so deserted. We wait for close to thirty minutes. To make a long story short, the company decided to lay off the entire team we'd been working with. Now, I'm not about to go criticizing a company's business decisions. They have the right to run their own company however they want. But as this senior VP is telling me all of this, my first response is empathy for the people I'd been working with, while my second response is to contemplate the huge amount of resources I'd allocated to the project. They owed a substantial amount of money.

Mister senior VP finishes his story and asks, "Do you have any questions?"

"Not at this time. Thank you."

What followed was a nerve-wracking series of phone calls. The first call was to our lawyer, who flat out told us he'd be lucky to negotiate half our due payment, minus the change order, which was now floating around in a corporate no-man's land unprocessed. Their lawyer called us and tried to strike a deal. At which point we told him he needed to talk to *our* lawyer. (Remember, kids: *lawyers* talk to *lawyers*.) And in an *amazing* stroke of luck one of the people the company had laid off had agreed to stay on for a few weeks to wrap things up. She reached out to us. Not only did she advocate for us, she tracked down the change order and made sure it was processed.

Amazingly, we got paid what was owed us. And it happened because we'd set up safeguards (our contract), matched their lawyer with our lawyer, and most importantly, had a strong advocate on the inside. Someone who was willing to go to bat for us because we'd been doing good work together. Without any of those three pieces I would not have made payroll and quite possibly would have had to lay people off myself.

We've already gone over how important a contract is in the design process, but a contract is a legal document that protects you when things go badly. Ultimately, you want things to go well, and you want to get paid for your work in a nice, timely fashion.

And before we go any further and everyone starts getting depressed, let's go over a few safety rules and reality checks. The vast majority of clients pay their bills. Most pay them on time. A small percentage pay late. And very few actually blow town without paying their bills. Everyone gets burned at least once. I've been burned a few times. If I hadn't been, I wouldn't know what to tell you.

The payment process is not so different from the design process itself in that you start by doing your research.

DO YOUR HOMEWORK

You have more power over how quickly you get paid than you might think. The first step is understanding everything that affects how soon you will get paid. Do your research and pay attention to details. And don't overlook the obvious.

Do they have money to pay you?

In the excitement to take on a project, and under the spell of the client's infectious charm and obvious passion for their project, you may forget to confirm whether they actually have the money to pay you. Watch out for this especially with startups and serial entrepreneurs—people who specialize in separating others from their money. Which is a fine skill. Just make sure they're doing it to multi-millionaire VCs and not to you.

"Our seed, first, second, etc., round is about to close," translates to "We don't *have* the money." As excited as you may be about working with someone, don't get yourself into a situation where getting paid depends on someone's funding coming through. That's not your fight. You already have one business to keep afloat.

Where is the money to pay you coming from?

Having money's not enough, though. It needs to be there when it's time to ante up, and it needs to be earmarked for you. Has the company set aside the budget for this project? Large organizations generally allocate budget before resources, so when GlobalMegaCo comes calling there's a good chance the budget's already been allocated. But when Joe'sNewNapkinIdeaStartup rings your bell, the money may or may not be there. It's up to you to find out for sure. How? Ask. There are two budget questions you need to ask during the biz dev process:

1. "What's your budget?"
2. "Has it been approved?"

If you feel weird about asking either of those questions, turn the book back to page one and start again. Keep doing that until you're comfortable talking about money.

If the client balks at answering either of those questions, you have a problem. Usually it'll be the first question that sticks in their craw. Some clients think that if you "trick" them into telling you their budget you'll tailor your estimate to it. You know what? They're right. If you tell me that you have $200K, and I feel it's appropriate, I'll show you what a $200K design solution looks like. If you have $40K, I'll see if I can come up with a $40K solution. But they'll be different solutions. I'm not going to charge you $200K for a $40K solution just because I know you have it. But the least helpful thing possible is for me to come up with a $200K solution when your budget is $40K. It wastes both our time. So tell me what your budget is and I won't show you the Audi on the lot when you have Civic money.

The more awkwardly you approach financial conversations with your client, the more awkward inexperienced clients will feel about answering them, and the less inclined more experienced clients will be to trust you.

Is there anything going on at the company that could result in the budget being yanked? Or even the company going away completely? How does their business work? Is it VC-backed, ad revenue, or subscription-supported? Is it a foundation sitting on a pile of cash socked away by robber barons a century or two ago? If the client is a VC-backed startup, when was their last round? Are you coming in at the beginning of a round, or toward the end? Does the board need to release the funds?

Some of this stuff is incredibly easy to find out. Heck, they'll just tell you most of it if you know to ask. In fact, asking these sorts of questions often inspires confidence in the client that they're hiring someone who knows how to ask the right questions. Some answers you can get from the news, blogs, or your vast network of connections. You might not get the answers to everything you need, but you can get most. And you'll certainly get more answers than you would by not asking.

THE INVOICE APPROVAL PROCESS

Once you determine that a company has the money to work with you, you need to find out who cuts the check. This is easier in small organizations, not impossible in others. But don't wait until a payment is actually late to do this. Do it as part of the project research.

What is the client's standard accounts payable process? (If there isn't one, it might be a good thing.) Do you need to watch a webinar to understand it?

Remember those movies you watched as a kid where they showed you where the milk came from? They'd start with a rooster crowing as the sun rose, and Farmer Bill walking to the barn carrying two buckets on his way to meet Bessie. Except that it turned out that Bessie was actually just what he called the incredibly complex equipment developed by the military that pumped a thousand cows simultaneously. And Farmer Bill sat in a windowed office overlooking the facility, his ass in an Aeron, reading *Moneyball,* manning a control panel that told him how much much milk was flowing and which cows were under-performing.

They would take you through each step of the process, following the milk from the cow to a pasteurization boiler, then poured into a bottle, capped, packed in a crate, loaded on a truck, unloaded at the supermarket, picked up by mom, and finally drunk by some little ginger kid.

Well, the invoice approval process is like that. (Shut up. I could have used the glue factory metaphor.) Only very rarely, in very small companies, does Client Bill take your invoice to his desk, pull out a checkbook, write you a check, and walk it back out to you. More often than not, your invoice is filtered through an onerous multi-step byzantine process, where at any juncture it can get misdirected, mangled, or simply disappear, never making its way back to your grubby little ginger hands.

It's in your best interest to find out exactly what kind of process your invoice needs to go through when it's submitted, who controls it at which juncture, how many steps are in between you and your bottle of milk, your options for receiving payment, and how they might go wrong. The more steps, the more potential bottlenecks.

Just as you design sites with actual people in mind and not for "users," you shouldn't try to get paid by Accounts Payable. You should try to get paid by Bob, or Dorothy, or Stella. As long as you treat Accounts Payable as another faceless process, they will treat you as another faceless invoice. Even the biggest, evilest corporation is staffed by moms and dads. Go make a friend! Share a milkshake together!

THE STRUCTURE OF THE ORGANIZATION IS THE BIGGEST DETERMINANT

Small companies tend to understand that other small companies need to get paid promptly. And you're much more likely to be working with, or at least have met, the person directly responsible for paying you. They may not even have a payment process at all, which goes one of two ways: you can convince them to pay you right away, which I wholeheartedly endorse, or your invoice sits forgotten on someone's desk. Or if they do have a payment process, it's just a matter of convincing the person a couple of cubicles over to move you to the front of the line.

Large organizations tend to have less flexible processes with more moving parts and less visibility into the people directly responsible for payment. It's not impossible to find them, mind you. But even if you make friends with Betty in Accounts Payable, which you should, she's not going to be able to change a large organization's accounting procedures by herself. She can, however, help you see into the process. She may also be an awesome resource for little hints and tricks that might speed things along.

Never, ever, go over Betty's head to get paid. You have messed with her world and she will hold up your invoices in perpetuity. Plus, it's a jerk move. And if you ever hope to work with this client again you'll forever have an enemy gatekeeper between you and your money.

Setting terms

For the uninitiated, "terms" refer to the agreement between you and your client about how long it'll take you to get paid. It is short for "terminal." As in the bus terminal you will end up sleeping in because you agreed to terms that weren't in your best interests and couldn't cover your rent.

Terms are referred to in wonderfully human terms such as net 15, net 30, net 45, and, for fans of comedy, net 60. (We once had a client try to talk us into net 90. It went as well as you'd expect it would go.) The number refers to the amount of time that can elapse between the date on your invoice and the date on the subsequent check. And the more institutional the client, the higher the number.

You've probably figured out that you want a lower number, like 15, to pay your bills, while your client wants a higher number, like 60, to to keep their money in the bank generating interest longer.

Don't settle for terms you're uncomfortable with. Negotiate. As always both parties will try to get the best terms for themselves. You propose 15, they counter with 60. So what do you counter with? 30? Who taught you to negotiate? You stick with your 15. Don't blink first. If you counter with 30 right away you'll get stuck at 45.

Remember, they're fighting for an extra 30 days of interest. You're fighting to stay in business. Which they'll need you to do to finish the project. It's in everyone's best interests to get you paid so you're focused on the work and not the finances. Never take on terms that put your business at risk.

There are other places to negotiate, apart from the net date. You can negotiate the number of payments. Sometimes lots of small payments are better than a few big ones. And a company may be able to give you better terms if your invoices fall below a certain amount. The larger the project, the more often I like to invoice, at smaller amounts. Otherwise you run the risk of going months without getting paid, and each possible late payment carries substantially more risk. You want to avoid a feast or famine scenario.

Beware of companies that treat paying you as a favor. You are delivering a valuable service for fair and agreed to compensation. If a potential client starts making cracks about money, get the hell out of there before it goes further. They're letting you know they don't value what you do. They will resent making payments.

Above all, never take on bad terms just to get a job. There are worse things than being poor. Namely, being poor *and* owing someone your time.

STRUCTURING PAYMENTS

We are in a special category of industry that gets paid a commencement fee, also called a deposit. It's an industry standard, and don't let anyone talk you out of it. Most clients have absolutely no problem with it. Others get a little weirded out. You know what? They're playing you against your inexperience.

Any industry that has to allocate a substantial amount of resources to create custom work, be they group resources or an individual's time, is taking a risk that needs to be mitigated by a deposit. Design is custom manufacturing. Anybody that's making something *specifically* for you, and tailored to your needs, is going to charge you a fee up front. What you're creating is not a commodity that can be turned around and sold to someone else. Your tailor, caterer, architect, the dude making uniforms for your little league team, the dopehead putting together your custom bike: all of these people are making things specifically for you. And if you should disappear on them the pool of people they can turn around and sell those items to is small to nonexistent.

If you go to your tailor and get fitted for a suit, he's gonna make a suit that fits you out of material you choose. (Notice how often I use tailor analogies? It's like a subliminal message.) If you decide to be a jerk and not show up to pick up that suit, he's stuck not only trying to find someone shaped just like you, but someone shaped just like you who has the same taste. That's gonna be next to impossible. He's not going to sink time into that. He's going to have to eat the suit. (Not literally, mind you. Unless your tastes are *really* peculiar.) To minimize his loss and to solidify your commitment he's going to ask you for a deposit. Now you both have skin in the game. He's sinking time and material; you've sunk some money. If your tailor is smart he'll negotiate for another payment from you during a fitting. That way he's covering his time spent on the suit at different stages, and minimizing potential losses. When the suit is finally finished, you make the last payment and take the suit. You also get a receipt, which in our little analogy is the equivalent of the intellectual property passing from the tailor to you.

Had I gone with a navigational analogy here, instead of a tailor analogy, I'd say that your tailor had tied knots in a rope as he uncoiled it. That way the rope can never unravel past the last knot. Seriously, you need a suit.

Make sure that your payments are tied to clear milestones. "When they're happy with the home page" is *not* a clear milestone. Tie it to an event that can be put on a calendar. Clients can argue whether something is approved or not far longer than they can argue whether a meeting ever happened. So if your milestone is the final design presentation you can invoice right after the meeting. Make sure the milestones are under your control. Unless you're responsible for a site going live, site launch is a horrible milestone.

Never tie a payment milestone to a metric. The world is an unsure place. And even when you do the research, the design, the development, and the testing correctly, things that are totally beyond your control can turn the world on its ear. You simply can't carry the brunt of that. As of this writing there has never been a federal bailout of small independent design studios and I'm not holding my breath.

At Mule we divide most projects into three or four payments. The commencement fee is due upon signing the contract. Don't kick off without it. If you do, you've lost all your leverage and it might as well be net 30. We don't walk into a kickoff meeting without a commencement check. The only exception is when we're working with a large company or organization (read: schools and state) where trying to meet that requirement puts an undue burden on the client. In those situations we wait until the payment has been processed. And we don't do that very often.

Feel free to tack on a late fee for late payment. Make sure it's high enough that you won't be upset if a company takes you up on it, and have it grow incrementally over a period of time.

DEALING WITH LATE PAYMENTS

Ninety percent of dealing with late payments is figuring out how to avoid late payments. So if you picked up the book and skipped right to this section because you've got an urgent problem, just hold on a sec. Yeah, I realize it's urgent. Yeah, I told you to chill a bit. Because I don't want you dealing with a late payment while your guns are hot.

The first rule of late payments is to remain calm. Under no circumstance should you go screaming angry into a client's office to get paid. Or start complaining publicly about it on Twitter. Those things may feel like the right thing at the time but neither of them get you any closer to your money.

Now that you're calm you can try to understand why the payment might be late. Just how late is it anyway? And where is it? Let's calmly track it down. Call your client. Remind them you were expecting payment and haven't received it. Ask them to acknowledge whether they've sent it. If they tell you they haven't, remind them it's due and ask them to put it in the mail that day. If they're local, offer to come get it or send a courier. It's worth $30 to get your money.

If they tell you they've sent it ask them for details: date sent, check number, tracking number if applicable.

Most late payments are a matter of disorganization. Very few are a matter of shame. (Ran out of money.) And even fewer are a matter of malice. (They just don't want to pay you.) Until you have evidence to the contrary, assume your missed payment is a matter of disorganization. That's the most likely possibility, and easiest to fix.

In large organizations, they might have a strict process, but release so many payments that some fall through the cracks.

Rapidly growing companies might have plenty of money but be totally disorganized about who and what needs paying.

True story: I once called a client about a late payment. They told me it had been mailed about a week before; gave me a check number and everything. I wasn't totally buying it, but played along and asked them to cancel that check and issue a new one. They helpfully agreed, and I ended the call feeling like the master negotiator that I obviously am. Well, as the master negotiator is coming back from lunch he decides to check the mail, and you got it, there was a now-cancelled check sitting there.

As for the late payments due to malice, or people just being jerks: these are the moments you save your lawyer for. Make every attempt to collect the amount owed you in good faith. And if that fails, unleash your lawyer. Just realize that he or she will charge you for getting that money, but 80% of a buck is still more than 100% of nothin'.

WHAT YOU CAN DO WHEN THE MONEY DOESN'T MATCH UP

In a crappy economy everyone pays late. Prepare for this. Negotiate smaller payments more often, so that each one isn't as big a hit and there's less time between them. Go into saving mode. Stash away as much money as possible. Client services is a land of feast and famine.

There will be times that your incoming cash flow won't be there in time to pay bills. Again, you should avoid this as much as possible by staggering your invoices and having a good mix of large and small invoices. Small jobs that pay faster and big jobs that pay more will diversify your payment schedule so that you have a steady stream of small payments coming in between the large ones.

But lean times will happen. Be ready for it by establishing a line of credit with your bank. I'll be honest with you, banks have been slashing lines of credits across the board. (Glad we bailed their asses out.) But if you're a business owner and you have a good relationship with your bank, walk in and ask; it's a common service. For good measure, try to make it at least two payrolls big.

CHIN UP, SPORT

Sadly, you will have to deal with people paying you late. There are things you can do to minimize that: enough research to know you're not getting into a bad situation to begin with, solid work, a good relationship with the client, a good contact in accounts payable, and a mutual understanding of what money is due when. Even then, things fall through the cracks and you'll need to use your knowledge of the situation to track down your payment. Help yourself get paid. I can't guarantee you'll never get screwed over again, but I'm pretty sure I can help you cut down on the times it happens.

And if you remember nothing else, don't walk away from money that's owed you. Go get it. You worked for it, you put in honest labor, and it deserves fair compensation. Get over your awkwardness with money. It's neither charming, nor "authentic." You're a professional designer, and professionals get paid.

I can't guarantee you that these conversations aren't hard. In fact I can vouch that they are. Being scared is generally a good sign that you're doing the right thing. I can, however, vouch that the second conversation you have about money will be easier than the first, and the third will be easier than the second, and so forth. Until one day you realize you're no longer scared to do it and you're writing a book about it.

10 WORKING WITH OTHERS

A LOT OF THIS BOOK has been about protecting yourself from other people. (The rest of it has been about protecting you from yourself.) So far we've dealt mostly with clients. But throughout your career, you're going to have to learn to deal with a multitude of other people to get your job done. Whether you work by yourself or as part of a team, knowing how to communicate with and listen to the other people around you will be a key factor to doing your job well.

Throughout your career you will deal with many different people, and they'll be driven by different things. I can give you a baseline for how to treat a client, or a co-worker, but ultimately you're going to have to figure out the best way to communicate with individual clients, and individual co-workers. And that takes listening, empathy, and understanding what drives people.

It takes confidence, self-awareness, and discipline to have good working relationships. You need to know what you want out of those relationships, know what the other person's concerns and anxieties are. And you need to have a clear understanding of how each of you fits into the process.

If you're working toward the same goals, respect each others' talent, time, and opinions, and you can figure out how to communicate what you need from each other to attain those goals, you'll do well. It also helps to know when to shut up. Be very clear and direct about what you need and you have a better chance of getting it.

WORKING WITH OTHER DESIGNERS

I took the bus to work this morning. It was rush hour, so I was packed in between other passengers in the very front, right by the driver. Another bus approached us from the opposite direction. The drivers made eye contact. They each lifted their hands to acknowledge each other, as if to say "Hello, I'm driving a bus, and so are you." The buses motored along. Within ten minutes each of them would pass by another bus and the scene would repeat itself.

Cabbies do the same thing. They'll also allow other cabbies to merge into traffic before them, which they'd never let another driver do, ever. And I imagine that bankers probably have a secret handshake when they run into each other in steam rooms. Just like Masons.

Most of the world's professions share a professional bond. At least enough of one to wave hello as they pass each other by and acknowledge that they're members of the same profession.

Designers, however, are another matter. If I am meeting with a client's team for the first time I can usually tell if they have a designer at the table. They're the one staring me down with a smirk on their face. Sizing me up. Probably wondering why I've been brought in to do a job they thought themselves perfectly capable of. This doesn't happen every time, of course. But it happens often.

So often that it needs to stop. Throughout my career I've heard the same complaint from almost every designer I've ever met: "No one values me." And throughout this book I've pointed out a myriad of reasons why this may be true, and how you've brought a lot of that on yourselves. And how it's within your power to fix it. And I'm telling you this with my heart full of love for you, for our craft, and for our profession. But until you start treating yourselves with respect, you can't expect others to do so. Until designers stop treating each other with the catty competitiveness of contestants in a trashy reality TV show, and start supporting each others' efforts, and figuring out how to complement each others' skill sets, you cannot expect others to take you seriously.

Until you stop throwing each other under the bus, no one will ever confuse you with the person driving it.

Better together

Working with other (talented) designers makes you a better designer, and is essential to your professional development, especially early in your career. There's simply no better way to learn your craft than to watch someone else practice it. But even as your career progresses, being in constant contact with someone else who speaks the same language will make you both better at what you do. Hell, just knowing that there's another designer in the room is sometimes enough to keep you from making lazy choices.

Working with designers that disagree with you is better than those who agree. They will make you fight over every decision you make! Which means you'll learn to come up with really tight rationales and really good work. If you can't get your work past another designer sitting right next to you, someone you trade jokes with every day, you're not going to get it past a demanding client.

Peer-to-peer criticism

Having other designers look at your work is different than getting client feedback. These are your people. You speak the same language. It's simultaneously more casual and more intense. After all, these are people who know you more intimately than your clients do. Maybe you work in the same space all day, maybe you meet up after work and show each other stuff. You're more willing to show them your mistakes, your lost causes, your uncertainties. At the same time, they're the people who know you're mailing it in, off the mark. They can not only tell you when something isn't working, but they can tell you *why* it's not working, and even tell you how to fix it. You need to take advantage of these people.

Perhaps this is a byproduct of the advancement of my own years, but lately I've noticed a trend away from criticism. The word itself makes designers do that unattractive pouting thing they do. How dare we criticize something that has been lovingly crafted by someone who had such pure intentions? Why be so harsh? We have begun defining our own work in such precious terms that even the hint of a dirty look might crush the little hollow bones that hold our designs together. We build each other up and pat each other on the back (gently!) for having the courage to have put our lovingly-crafted pixels on screen for those who know how to appreciate their delicacy.

Not only have we have forgotten how to use power tools, we've begun confusing building IKEA shelves with furniture-making.

"But I worked so hard on this!"

Before this whole "design thing," I had the pleasure of disappointing my parents, hard-working immigrants that they were, by going to art school. We were taught to express ourselves, bear our souls, develop our own personal vocabularies and read terrible, terrible French literature. And once a week we would get together and critique each other's work. We'd line up all these highly personal artifacts we'd supposedly poured our souls into, and spend the day seeing who could come up with the most brutal takedowns. We'd eviscerate each other. It didn't matter whether the work was done by a friend or someone you didn't know. The task was two-fold: build critical thinking skills and thick skin.

But this house of horrors had rules. You could say anything you wanted about the work itself, the effort that went into the work, and the craft of execution, but if you made a personal comment about the author the room would stop dead in its tracks. You'd be asked to leave. You simply did not criticize an individual. If you were going to make someone cry, which happened multiple times a day, you had to do it because they were a bad artist, not a bad person.

Now mind you, I am not trying to make a connection between art and design. The two couldn't be more different: one is a corporate business tool for manipulating the poor, and the other is design. But there is a connection to be made between those critiques and peer-to-peer criticism. A few months in and something started to happen in those critiques. First off, people left. Having your work regularly criticized by your peers is hard. But those who stayed watched their work get better. And their critical skills improved as well. By the end of the year, we were not only doing better work, our critical thinking skills were sharp as knives.

Sorry for the art analogy. Let's get back to the office.

I'll concede the point that going into work every day to be criticized by your peers is not very pleasant. And it's certainly not going to work out unless you lay some ground rules. It works if everyone involved respects one another. It works when there's a sense of decorum. You have to talk about the work, not the person doing the work. And you have to recognize that everyone involved in critiquing the work has the best interests of both the project and the designer in mind. (If they don't, you have a bigger problem.)

Start be clearly defining the goals at hand. Discuss whether the goals were met and how well. Even good work can be better. The goal is never to make something good enough. The goal is also never to work hard on something. The goal is always to get it right. (Do not confuse someone having worked hard on something with it being right!)

As the person being critiqued, you need to realize that the feedback is not about you, it's about the work. And you need to be open to good ideas that come from places other than your own head. There's a balance between defending your work and remaining open to better ideas that takes a long time to develop. It takes confidence, intelligence, and an open mind to allow others to help you make your work better. It takes a thick head not to.

No more catty competition

The perception (or reality) of competition poisons the working relationship between designers.

As a designer working in client services we're often brought into situations where there's a designer on the client team. You'd be amazed at how often their existence is hidden from us. I'm not quite sure who the client is attempting to protect in these situations: us, the designer, or more likely themselves.

We're often brought in after a job has been attempted internally. This is a tough situation for everyone. The internal designer might feel threatened that someone else is now in charge of a job they couldn't do. (More likely they didn't have the internal support to get it done.) At times the internal designer has lobbied not to have an external team brought in and lost. Also awkward.

Funny story. We're about a month into a project with a client. Redesigning an online service. I'm sitting in the client's office and we're batting around a few ideas that have come up. I mention a particular flow I'm considering. "That sounds like something Sam came up with a while back?"

"Who's Sam?"

"He's a designer that was on this project for a few months. Came up with a few ideas. Other stuff came up though."

"Can I talk to him?"

"Knock yourself out."

The next day I go looking for this Sam, chat him up, he digs around his desk and pulls out a full set of flows and page schematics for the product we're working on. And there were some very good ideas in there. To make a long story short, we got Sam involved in the project and a huge percentage of what we ended up designing had its genesis in those wireframes of his. Rather than reinventing a solution from scratch, we used his vast knowledge of the product and ideas that he had already explored and took them further than either of us could have done separately.

And finding out about him was total happenstance.

If you're on the services side, make sure to find the client's internal designers. Their internal knowledge will be a fantastic resource to someone coming in cold. If you're an internal designer and a design team is brought in, reach out to meet them. Their status as outsiders will make it possible for them to navigate above the company's internal politics. Swallow your pride. You can both do things the other can't. Together you're a stronger team than you are apart.

Sam could have been totally pissed off that someone else had been brought in to work on a project he'd done some really excellent thinking on. We could have been threatened that Sam had not only already done all of this work, but that our thinking was taking us down the same path. Instead, we realized we both understood the problem the same way and decided to tackle the problem together. Not to mention the company was open-minded enough to let us do so.

Whether you are thrown together on the same project or accidentally discover yourselves on the same project, you're all better off uniting behind a common goal than you are competing for attention and resources.

My first art director

More often than not, though, the situation above plays itself differently. Designers are a maddening combination of competitiveness and insecurity. For every story I have about someone like Sam, I have ten stories about walking into a client's office to find them looking at a competing comp from an internal designer. And I'll freely admit to you that before I knew better, I was the one making the competing comps when my own boss hired from the outside. Why did I do this? Easy. I felt like I was better than the designers that had been brought in. And more importantly, I was afraid I wasn't.

Like all animals we crave validation. I didn't care *what* my boss thought of those other designers as long as he thought *better* of me. I was very lucky to meet a designer named Matt early in my career. Matt was brought in to do an annual report that my boss didn't think I was ready to do. (For what it's worth I would have *nailed* it, dick!) From the moment he came in I was irritated. He could sense it; I'm not very good at hiding when I'm irritated. So one day Matt invites me to lunch and we start talking design. He starts asking me about the company. And starts running ideas for the annual report by me. Next thing you know we're working on it together. He's giving me tasks. We're giving each other feedback. He was, for all intents and purposes, my first art director. And he taught me what you could accomplish working toward the same purpose, rather than trying to undermine each other.

So now when I walk into a situation and find another designer in the position that I was in, I reach out to them. Like Matt did. We are all links in a continuous timeline of a shared craft. It is our responsibility to keep that timeline strong. To add to it. To pull the next link aboard.

Act like it's within your power to improve your relationship with other designers and you usually can.

The "rules" of working with other designers

Respect

You can't work with people you can't respect. Yet I fear that too often we choose not to respect people simply because their ideas, their viewpoints, and the way they approach a problem is different than ours. And that means we're cheating ourselves out of a new (or old!) way to solve a problem. There's always something to be learned from working with another designer, whether they're a grizzled veteran or a fresh face.

Remember those print designers we used to laugh at? Well, the web finally caught up to where everything they knew about layout, color theory, and typography was essential. We weren't doing anything new with design. Our technology just hadn't caught up to what design was capable of yet.

Getting good at doing what you love means having the confidence to recognize what you know, the humility to recognize what you don't, and the courage to extend our respect to those who make our faults more visible.

Clear roles

To work together without tripping over each other and duplicating each others' efforts you need to establish clear roles. Decide who owns what. Decide how feedback is going to work. Depending on the circumstances, a communication chain with the client may be in order. And yes, one of you may have to be in charge. (More on that later.)

Remember the bus drivers at the beginning of the chapter? How well do you think they'd all get along if they decided to start driving each other's routes because they felt they could do a better job?

Hard is it may be, once you decide another designer owns a particular piece of the problem, you need to trust them with it. Communicate often. Give each other honest feedback. If their work is sucking, let them know, and work out other possible solutions together. But under no means should you "surprise" another designer with your take on something they own. And trust me, as someone who works with other designers, it is so very, very hard to not grab that mouse away sometimes. I'll know exactly how to fix something, and we'll be talking it through, and my hand starts slowly working its way to their mouse. That's a terrible urge though. It's disrespectful of the other designer. It's a wasted teachable moment. And above all, it's a sign you don't trust your feedback skills as much as your execution skills.

The goals of the project come first

Whose idea was it? Who cares, if it's a good idea. If everyone on the team can rally around a common goal the chances of achieving that goal increase exponentially. If we're spending time debating whether the map transition was Jim's idea or

Betty's idea, we're not implementing the map transition. What matters is that we have a good idea to implement.

Whether you are working with other designers on your team or designers on a client team, you will ultimately be judged on the success of the overall project rather than individual achievements. So why let ego and pettiness spoil the party?

You can learn to feed your ego family-style when you celebrate the completion of a successful project along with everyone else.

When I look back at projects I've worked on, the ones that stand out are the ones where people worked well together, not the ones where individual ideas and achievements stand out. And the halo over a successful project tends to encompass the entire team.

Remember that Jordan won no rings until he learned to distribute the ball and involve his teammates. Once he did he won six.

Don't drive someone else's route

Every once in a while we get a potential new client who tells us they'd like to hire us because they're not happy with their current firm. Or they're "disentangling themselves" from their current firm. Or they're not happy with what their current firm is doing and they want us to review their work. We turn those clients down. You should as well. Never step on another designer's work. Anything you say about that firm's work will be used against them. It's one thing to compete honestly for projects, it's another thing altogether to have a hand in getting another designer fired.

If a client's not happy with the firm they hired, let them clean it up. You stay clear of that mess.

The same goes for that horrid practice of posting *your* version of a redesign that has just gone live. By all means, critique it. Write about what works and doesn't work, but keep in mind that another designer was working under constraints and internal politics that you may not be aware of. So write up your thoughts as a user, even as a user who's also a designer.

But taking the time to redo their work and posting it publicly is smug and petty. (Yes, it's happened to me. Yes, I'm still annoyed about it.)

Stand united. Or I will yell at you.

But hey, it takes more than designers to make stuff happen, right? Let's meet some of those other people.

THOSE OTHER PEOPLE IN THE OFFICE

Working with other people is simple: figure out what they want, and make sure they understand what *you* want. The rest is a rounding error.

A few years ago, during my company's infancy, I was totally addicted to a TV show on the Discovery Channel (the monkeys and hammers channel) called *Monster House*. The premise in a nutshell: Steve, the foreman, would assemble a group of contractors, each with a different specialty, and they'd have a week to completely redo part of someone's house. During the week the contractors would bicker. Yet somehow at the end they always pulled through and the owners of the house would either be delighted or pissed that there was a fire-shooting fountain in the living room and a moat where their lawn used to be.

But the part of the show I enjoyed most (or at least that serves our purposes today) was the very beginning. Steve the foreman would gather his whole crew together in a room and go over ideas for what they could do. Everyone worked together on this. The carpenter would suggest a drawbridge in the backyard, the general contractor would weigh in on how to do that while taking out 75% of the house's load-bearing walls, and the electrician would estimate how much power to steal from the neighborhood grid to make it work.

And I turned to my partner Erika and said, "*That's* how we need to work! We need to involve everyone in the project from the very beginning."

And that is how we work. At the beginning of every project, all the members of the team get together and throw out ideas. There's a fantastic amount of energy in the room as we simultaneously debate how to organize, design, and build things. As we go, we check on whether someone's idea might take us over budget, or blow our deadline, while our lead researcher points out that no one wants a website with a fire-breathing fountain.

That way, when we all head off to our own specialties, we're doing it with a group agreement on what it is we're going to build.

I've worked at too many places where page schematics were thrown on my desk, fully formed, and comps delivered to developers as a fait accompli, often being seen for the very first time, to tell you that it *does not work!*

If you have the luxury of working in a room full of designers of all specialties, you need to make full use of them. Work together. Early and often. Share in the failures and successes. But I guarantee, if you find people you work well with, the successes will outweigh the failures.

Depending on where you work, you might have a multitude of other people in the office. Even if you work alone out of your studio apartment you'll undoubtedly have to interact with other people (other craftspeople!) at some point during the day.

We've already gone over clients at length, as well as lawyers and obviously other designers. But web design is a complex thing. Lots of moving parts. And all of those parts require a person who's really good at that particular skill.

If you're in a small company many of these roles may be filled by the same person. If you're in a large company, each of these roles may be further broken down into mind-numbing sub-specialties.

They're as responsible for the success of projects as you are. And as deserving of your respect as you are of theirs.

Project managers

You know what's great about project managers? They manage projects. They keep things on time and on budget. They allocate resources and make sure you're working on what you need to be working on. They do this by carefully lining up all the pieces that make a project go. They spend a great deal of time creating intricate timelines to ensure a project gets done on time, and when everything shifts, they do it again.

Just as you're responsible for the quality of a project, your project manager is responsible for getting it done on time. And with the maximum amount of profit. This doesn't mean you're not both thinking about those things. It means you each own your part of the project. This often leads to tension, as your ultimate goal is to do good work, and the project manager's ultimate goal is to do the work on time. And that's pretty much how it should work. With each party pushing for the piece they own, and playing against each other, you can deliver excellent work on time.

The project manager also serves as the voice of the client in the room. They make sure the client's requirements are being met, and do most of the day-to-day checking in with the client.

Project managers are not your mother. They may be the project's mother, but not yours. They're not there to manage you, outside of how you fit into whatever project they're managing.

The best way to work with a project manager is to be clear about what each of you are responsible for and to keep them informed of project process as much as possible. Don't wait until you've missed a deadline to alert your project manager to a problem. As soon as you get an inkling that you're going to blow a deadline, let them know. Help them help you by giving them enough time to triage the problem with the client.

There may be times when you feel like you and the project manager are working in total opposition, but you're not. You're working toward the same goal—you just have different ways to get there.

You can also make their lives easier (and by extension, yours) by cutting the "creative" routine. Be realistic about your time estimates, mind your deadlines, understand the scope. Be someone who can be counted on.

Researchers

A good researcher will make sure you're not building houses with basements in a flood zone. They run interviews with the client's team and with potential customers. They review the client's analytics. Their job isn't to tell you what to design; after all, no researcher could have told Henry Ford that people wanted cars. But a good researcher could have told him that people enjoyed going faster.

Much as the project manager serves as the voice of the client in the room, the researcher functions as the voice of the user. A good researcher will talk directly to the people the work you're doing is intended for and find out about their habits and proclivities. Good research is invaluable in knowing whether you're headed down the right design path.

You should make it a habit to sit in on as many of these interviews as possible. It'll give you a much better sense of who you're designing for.

Research doesn't tell you *how* to design, it tells you *where* to design. And a good researcher isn't prescriptive, they just gather and analyze the data. It's your job to figure out what to do with it. Frequent check-ins with your researcher throughout the design process can be incredibly helpful to validate your decisions against their research.

The success of *every* project depends on how well it resonates with its intended audience. And your researcher is your eye into that audience. Treat them well.

Information designers

An information designer, or information "architect," is a type of designer. You may even be one! (Short aside: I hate the term "information architect"; it's a shame phrase, like "graphic novels." Designers are designers.) They figure out the structure of things: how everything fits together, how to get from point A to point B, taxonomies, organizing principles, categories, etc. Basically, they figure out where things live and how you get to them.

Information designers flesh out the structure and underlying principles of the site, i.e., the blueprints (thus the architect thing). This is generally borne out in wireframes, also known as page schematics.

A client should sign off on the underlying structure of the site in a bare-bones wireframe before being shown a presentation layer; that way, we collect agreements at various stages along the way, and things can only unravel as far as the last point of agreement. Like tying knots in a rope.

This doesn't mean the visual designer is sitting on his hands until the information designer gets that sign-off. Optimally, the two parties work as closely as possible to come up with possibilities and then go off to execute their individual pieces. Solve together, execute apart.

For years I worked in various places where information designers would work away, headphones on, uninterruptible, and then drop a hundred or so wireframes on my desk. Depending on the information designers, these wireframes would be in several states of fidelity, from pencil sketches, to fully fleshed-out page mockups. They would then disappear into their next project. This is known as "waterfall" development. Because you'd want to put them in a barrel and throw them over a waterfall.

My preferred method of working with information designers is to set up in front of a large whiteboard and diagram what we're working on together. The earlier you start developing solutions in common the better the project goes. And whiteboards make for easy and quick revisions. We take lots of pictures. And at some point you'll need to go back and document all of that stuff for the sake of the client. But the more you check in with each other and review each others' work while it's in progress, the more likely you'll head toward a strong solution you both agree on.

Who owns layout? Solving this problem once and for all

Every day, all across the world, probably as you read this, there's a designer presenting page schematics, or wireframes, to a client. A page schematic is a terribly confusing thing to be showing to someone who's not trained to read them. Even for someone who runs a website. (Ever look at the electrical wiring diagram for a refrigerator? Yet you stick your arm in one multiple times a day.)

And as if showing them that very confusing document isn't enough pain to begin with we also throw in the biggest lie we tell our clients every day:

"These don't imply layout."

Oh, for fuck's sake. How could they *not?*

This is generally done as a way to leave enough leeway for the visual designer to then come in and have the freedom to move things around as they organize the space and begin creating a visual experience. Which, by the way, we love. I once worked with an information designer who yelled at me for "moving things around!" (She's no longer with us. The industry, I mean. Nothing was ever proven.) But we're passing the problem on to our clients. We simply can't tell a client to ignore the most obvious thing in front of them: an organized box! And think of all the meeting time we'd save by not having to constantly repeat that stupid phrase.

For years we'd go back and forth on ideas to make the river run uphill, and, well, the metaphor just gave it away. Let layout be layout. Get the visual designer and the information designer working together from the start. Get them to agree on a basic grid, a potential layout, core functionality placement, etc. And have everyone evolve that idea as the project moves forward so that every party is aware of what's going on.

That way when you're putting something in front of a client you can say something more to the tune of "This is where we're headed with the layout, which we're evolving together."

So who owns layout? You all do. Now can we please stop arguing about it? It's exhausting.

Developers

If you're a web designer, you should know how to code. However, if like me you have the luxury of working with fantastic developers, you may find your own hands-on skills getting rusty, even as you stay on top of all the ridiculously amazing advances in our field over the last few years.

Of all the other people in the office, I work closest with the developers, because until we start making actual code, we're looking at paintings of websites. We work back and forth at a pretty fast pace, riffing on each others' work as we go. I don't hand them things to build, we work on things to build together. The sooner we get into code, the sooner we can start iterating.

For example, we're loving responsive design, right? And just this week I started mocking up the full-width desktop version of a site, and as soon as we'd agreed on the basic framework, my developer, Jim Ray, took that and started working through the responsive stuff. But every fifteen minutes or so, one of us would have to adjust what we were doing because the other one had either found a problem, or a better way to do something. We were making quicker and better decisions because design and development were informing each other. Had I attempted to mock up all of those responsive states and then hand them to Jim to code, those mistakes would have been baked in, and we would have spent days trying to chase them down. Not to mention that we would have probably asked the client to approve the final design, and it would have been broken.

We often comp just enough to figure out what it is we're building, which is why we don't include Photoshop comps with our final deliverables. They're a mess, and often an unfinished mess which may have little resemblance to what we ended up building. Don't spend time updating paintings when what the client paid for was a website.

Engineers

Engineers build the things you design. They come in many flavors, such as application engineers, web developers, and software engineers. They're often bundled together as "backend" engineers.

Some people also refer to developers as frontend engineers. I pulled developers out separately because they work so closely with designers, and in many cases the designer *is* the developer, that I think the relationship is different. Although the more a developer starts moving into programming languages such as JavaScript, Ruby, PHP, and Python, the more likely they'll start referring to themselves as an engineer (and requesting a higher salary).

You've probably heard the phrase "designed by engineers"? They probably like to say things like "engineered by designers."

During my days in the startup salt mines a long, long time ago, I was working on a product redesign for a company I'd just joined. The design team was working through a new signup flow. I was arguing that step three needed to come before step two. (I can't remember if I was right anymore, but let's assume I was.) The rest of the team, who'd all been there longer, were arguing that the steps couldn't be swapped because it wasn't engineered that way. I hate hearing a designer argue against something not because it's right or wrong, but because it means a possible hard conversation. Hate it. So I said, "Let's go talk to engineering."

"You can't!"

"Why not?"

And I realized no one on that team had ever had a discussion with anyone in engineering about a product while they were still working on it. Things were delivered in a final state, engineering put it all together, often revising design decisions on the fly because of constraints we didn't know (or hadn't asked!) about, and both fiefdoms co-existed peacefully.

The next day I invited the lead engineer to lunch and afterward asked if we could swing by my desk so I could show him something. I walked him through the new signup flow. With step three before step two.

"That's not how we do it now," he said.

I explained that I thought the new flow would lead to a higher conversion rate because it moved the credit card fetching to the end, front-loading the rest of the user data, and meaning people had more skin in the game and were slightly less inclined to bail.

He agreed it was a good idea. At which point we presented the idea to the head of product *together*.

And from that point forward we had regular check-ins with engineering. And it was much less likely that design would be changed in engineering, because we were catching the problems together and avoiding them.

Seasoned engineers tend not to go for trendy ideas, and have a lot of experience making pragmatic decisions. They are very good at what they do, as are you. And you'll find that if you explain your rationale for your design decisions—as you need to be able to do with anyone you work with—they are an incredible resource. But as long as you're both on separate sides of the gym thinking each other is weird, no one gets to dance.

There's a tendency for designers to think of what they do as "hard" because it's so subjective, and of engineering as "easy" because there's a "right" answer. But I can assure you that there's as much, if not more, creativity in how an engineer solves a problem as in how a designer does.

Marketers

I've always been one to believe that all design is marketing. A well-designed chair summons your ass to it, a well-designed bike makes even the most honest among us want to steal it, and a well-designed website makes you want to use it. So why does "marketing" leave such a bad taste in designers' mouths? Well, because most of it is bad.

There are good marketers and bad marketers, just like there are good designers and bad designers. A good marketer works for your audience. A bad marketer works for your advertisers. A good marketer will work with you to put together the best possible experience for your customers. Their main concern is making sure that the site stays in business so those customers can get their needs met. The easiest way to tell if you're working with a bad marketer is to ask them, "Can you please explain what that means?" after they've said something. If they can't, put a stake through their heart.

Put a bad designer and a bad marketer together and you will get exponential crap. You'll also get a ton of complaining on both sides. And it will all boil down to, "this other person isn't making me good at my job." Put a good marketer and a good designer together and they'll achieve things neither of them could by themselves.

So as designers I'd like to implore you to do a few things. First off, stop having a knee-jerk response to marketing. Search out the good ones and work with them. Second, accept the fact that you also work in marketing. You are creatures of persuasion by nature. Just persuade people to do better things. Start with yourselves.

If you're tired of marketing $200 basketball shoes to poor kids, then figure out what it is you *want* to persuade people to do, and go do that. Get a good marketing person to help you.

Content strategists

I saved my favorite for last. There's been a resurgence in content strategy lately that's been a joy to behold, in part. On the one hand, I'm thrilled people are talking about it and advancing its cause. On the other hand, there's a tendency to treat it as a new craft, which reminds me of when web designers first launched Photoshop and thought they'd invented design. Content strategy has certainly been an underserved craft, but it's hardly new to the world, much less the world of the web.

Since we're now far along in the book I believe I can give you some bad news. Almost no one is coming to the sites you work on because of your excellent design work, and those few that do are there to steal. People show up for the *stuff*. Design makes the stuff easy to find, and a pleasure to use; but it's not the stuff. The web is made of content. Design is what holds all that content in place.

Don't feel bad; the Golden Gate Bridge is only there to help cars get across, but it's the bridge that people photograph.

Content strategists help clients organize and plan for all of that stuff. If you have a content strategist at your disposal, start working together early and often. (That seems like a repeating theme. Weird.) You can't build a container for something if you don't know what size it is.

There are two holy questions of any type of design: who is it for? And what are you putting in it? Content strategists are a godsend in figuring out the latter question. And that answer needs to inform what you're designing. You can't shove a silverback into a cat carrier.

ON FINDING YOURSELF IN CHARGE

I once had the pleasure of working with a very talented in-house designer at a large internet company. Let's call him Bob, because everyone in this book is named Bob. Bob was a talented, good-natured guy. He knew his way around the company. He was always eager to help. And he had good ideas. I liked working with Bob.

One day, toward the end of the project, I'm having lunch with Bob in the company's luxurious subsidized cafeteria. I was having the swordfish. Bob says there's an opening for a design director and he's thinking about applying.

I encourage him to do so; after all, he's talented, good with people, and well-respected within the company. He appreciates my encouragement and decides to apply.

A few weeks later we're back at our studio, having finished the project, and I get an email from Bob telling me he got the job. I reply my congratulations back to him, excited that his confidence and hard work paid off.

About a year later we got another contract with the same company. Unfortunately, we weren't working with Bob this time, but I searched him out. Bob looked like a different person. He had circles under his eyes, his skin was a whitish green, and his studio was packed with piles of paperwork.

"How are you Bob? Wanna grab lunch?"

Over lunch Bob described how his work life had turned into an endless task of scheduling designers on projects, attending management meetings, scheduling vacations, and office politics.

"And I don't get to design anything anymore," he said.

Corporate status vs. professional development

Bob's story is sad, and not uncommon. I have way too many friends who've chased jobs because they were the next logical step in building a résumé. And obviously climbing the corporate ladder comes with a higher salary. We can't begrudge anyone the opportunity to make a better living.

But does the cost of making a better living have to mean giving up doing the thing you love doing? And how smart is a company that elevates people out of the thing they do best? There's got to be a better way to reward people while leveraging their talent.

As your career advances it makes sense to take on more and more responsibility. And to make more money for doing so. But do you want to be in charge of the work or the people? Of all the people I know who've taken a job because it came with a "title," even while they knew they wouldn't be doing the kind of work they wanted to do, I can't think of one that looks back on that as a good decision. Not a one.

So as your career develops you will be faced with the choice of how to take it to the next level. Do you start your own company? Do you aim for design director at a large firm? Do you become a well-sought consultant where you only work six months of the year out of your swank modernist home in the hills?

The choice is yours. But I'd caution you to stay away from jobs that take you away from the thing you love to do, which is to design things. Although your definition of "designing things" may change. My friend John Gruber once said that Steve Jobs' greatest accomplishment wasn't designing any particular Apple product—it was designing Apple itself. At some point you may get to the point where you're no longer designing specific products, or specific websites, but instead helping to design the teams that design those things. And eventually designing the companies that those teams design within. But you don't stop designing.

If you're at a company where the next step up the ladder means managing people more than managing the quality of the design the company is producing, get the hell out of there.

There's way too much design to be done to be losing good people to idiotic corporate structures that take our best designers out of commission. There are people who love managing people and scheduling their vacations. Leave that to them.

Directing others

Even the Greatest Designer Of all Time™ can only work so fast and do so much work. Eventually, either you'll be so successful that you'll have to figure out a way to increase your output without going nuts, or your company will decide that you're too much of a valued commodity to do the job of one person. Which means hiring other designers. Which means you're now directing them. The best way to get more value out of a designer who's reached a certain level is to have them teach what they know to other designers. (Just make sure you're in charge of their work quality, not their administrative overhead.)

I've been directing other designers at Mule for years. I absolutely sucked at it at first. (At least ten people just whispered, "You *still* suck at it.") It takes a while to get past your own competitive nature and inclination to just grab someone's mouse and say "Step aside!" Because, honestly, you probably *can* do what you're asking them to do a lot faster and most likely a lot better. But you'll be condemning yourself to a situation where you'll always have to jump in and be Batman, saving the city at the last minute from an inept police force, most likely made more inept because they know you'll swoop in when you're needed. (Ever wonder why Batman didn't just open up a secret facility and have Jim Gordon send him his best cops for some intensive training time? Because Batman has a huge ego is why.)

The first rule of directing others is that you have to let go of that ego. Or at least redirect it. The game is no longer about how well *you* can design something, it's about how well you can work with others so that you can design well together. Otherwise you'll be stuck in a situation where your capacity is limited to what you yourself can produce.

Not to mention being limited to ideas which only you can think of. The biggest joy for me in directing other designers is seeing them come up with ideas which I would have never come up with, and then working together to help them bring those ideas to fruition.

Give your people enough leeway to fail. And not so you can swoop in and save them, but specifically so they can trust that you *won't*. They need to learn to fall before they learn how to recover.

The designers you're directing need to be willing to show you work in progress. This isn't a presentation situation; this is intimate. This is sometimes looking over the shoulder stuff. You know how much people like having someone hover over their shoulder? Not at all. Which means you need to establish trust. On both sides. Which means when you're looking over your designer's shoulder you're the *only* one looking over her shoulder. Not you and the project manager, not you and the whole team. Just you. Your designers need to feel secure enough to tell you when they're stuck. And trust you enough to help them get unstuck.

People at different levels need to be directed differently. A younger, less experienced designer will need more frequent check-ins and more prescriptive feedback, while a more experienced designer may just need the occasional course-correction. But even more than that, a good design director will find out the best approach for each of the people he or she is responsible for.

But none of this works if people aren't willing to be directed. And if you aren't strong enough to do it. We've had designers come to work for us who'd either never been directed by anyone before, or had been damaged by bad design directors in the past. In both cases, you have to be up front and direct with them about how your relationship is going to work and who's in charge. They need to understand when it's ok to push back and when to acquiesce and just start doing what you tell them to, because that moment does come. Ultimately, you have a responsibility to deliver good work to your client. So training less experienced designers needs to be done within a setting where the client work doesn't suffer as a result. You can't deliver work with training wheels.

The most dangerous instance in directing someone comes when you and they don't agree about their skill level. A young designer who believes they're better than they actually are won't be as open to your direction. They'll fight you and get defensive. Rather than being open-minded about the problem you're currently pointing out, they'll be wondering why you see a problem at all. They've closed themselves off to being directed and that relationship isn't going to work.

Before we hire designers at Mule, I'm very clear with them about where I think they are talent and experience wise. I also tell them where I expect those skill levels to be in six months, and how we'll get them there. If they agree with the assessment and can commit to the work required to meet those future expectations, then we hire them. And with every designer I hire I'm always looking for the one who's eventually going to take over my job.

Being the boss

There are people for whom leadership comes naturally. I'm not one of them. I started my own company because I wanted to be able to choose the types of jobs I worked on, because I was arrogant enough to think I could do it, and honestly, because I didn't realize how hard it would be. And maybe that was a good thing.

You know those cautionary signs you see all over the place, the ones with great graphics of a mangled hand going between two cogs or someone's hair getting caught on a fence? And you wonder what event caused those signs to be posted? This book is a collection of those signs. Every lesson contained in here was hard-won. And none was harder than the lesson of learning how to be in charge.

Whether you're the lead designer on a project, or the director of a group of designers, or the head of the company, or the captain of a ship, your team's success is dependent upon strong leadership.

I love bad TV. And for a while I was addicted to this ridiculous show called *Whale Wars* where a ship full of well-meaning hippies and trust fund babies getting back at their parents chased the Japanese whaling fleet around the South Seas. If ever a show had clearly defined "good guys" and "bad guys," this was it. Whales are awesome. No one wants to see a dead whale being pulled onto a ship and gutted. It's awful. And here were these well-meaning, if patchouli-stinking, kids primed to be the good guys.

But the captain of the hippie ship was a terribly inept leader. He was unable to make decisions. He made passive-aggressive comments to his crew. And ultimately he locked himself away in his quarters during the climactic episode of the season while telling his crew to handle the situation themselves. They were lost. They were looking for leadership that just wasn't going to come. And that's a horrible feeling. By the end of the series I was actively rooting for the Japanese whalers to take their boat down. I am a terrible person, but the whales deserved a better champion.

Luckily, we don't work on ships and we're not bound to maritime law, so I can tell you that sometimes you need to just become the leader you're looking for without leaving yourself open to a mutiny charge.

Flat hierarchies are a lie

We're not complex creatures. We're chimps who know HTML5. And like chimps, we need to know someone is in charge. We get uneasy when the hierarchy is in flux. And we feel secure when our leadership is confidently taking us in the right direction. We like knowing what we're responsible for, and whether we're doing it well, or whether we're doing it badly—especially if it also comes with instructions on how we can do it well instead. We like being rewarded in front of the other chimps, and being reprimanded behind the dignity of closed doors. We like to know whether we're doing our jobs well from the person, or chimp, who entrusted us with them.

When we first started hiring people, I was happy to let them find their way. Or, better said, I was too insecure in my own leadership abilities to point them in a particular direction. I was trying to be their buddy. Their fellow designer. They were looking for clear expectations on how to succeed. From their boss. And I failed them.

People *want* to do well. They need goals to meet. And you need to set those goals.

Hire people smarter than you

Everyone says this, but it's hard to do. It's much easier to hire people who are *almost* as smart as you, smarter than you at something you don't like doing, or (my all-time favorite) remind you of yourself at a younger age. But to actually hire people smarter than you requires a heck of a lot of confidence and self-awareness.

Think of it this way, though: there are going to be people smarter than you out there. Where do you want them? Working for you, or for someone else? And surrounding yourself with smart, talented people is only going to make you better. It's certainly the right call for the sake of the team.

And if you're honestly trying to build a team of incredibly smart people, be content that your place in the group doesn't have to be as the smartest one. You only need to be smart enough to convince them to work for you and keep them engaged.

Learn how to apologize

We've screwed up a lot over the years, but one particular screw-up stands out. Not because of the screw-up itself, but because of the way it was handled. Which I'd love to tell you was totally thought out, but it wasn't. That's how all of these lessons go: you screw up, you stumble into solutions, and you remember them.

Anyway, we'd messed something up and the client was on the phone. He was pretty unhappy and verging on irate. Our project manager was attempting to placate him. She was explaining it wasn't actually that bad, that we'd fix it, these things happen, etc. She was doing her job well. And offering him everything she was able to. Finally he asks to speak to me. I pick up the phone. He's mad. He explains the problem. And I reply: "This is my responsibility. I apologize. It won't happen again. Now what can we do to fix it?"

Did we actually screw up? Who knows. But I realized that the only way we could get past his anger was to apologize. And that's not something I could ask someone else to do, nor would he have accepted it from someone else. And, quite honestly, as the boss that was my sword to fall on.

You're going to screw up. Big. And when you do you need to own it, clean it up, and move on. I've never held a mistake against an employee, but I can't tolerate someone who's unable to admit to their mistake. And when it's a client-facing mistake you, as the boss, need to raise your hand and claim it.

Know when to part ways

If you think this section is about firing people you're only partially right. That's coming up. But I recently said goodbye to one of my favorite designers I've ever worked with. She was talented, good-natured, smart, and a pure joy to work with. But she realized it was time to go do her own thing. And as sad as I was when she told me she was leaving, I was just as thrilled to hear she was confident enough to go at it on her own.

If you hire the right kind of people, they will eventually either leave you, or try to displace you. (My curse is not having been able to find the latter.)

Unfortunately, there are times when parting ways isn't such a happy event. Sometimes you hire the wrong people. Sometimes you hire good people and it turns out you just can't work together. There are lots of ways for relationships to go beyond fixing. And only one way to fix the problem. Being in charge means that every once in a while you're going to have to fire someone.

There's more pleasant names for it, of course: letting them go, telling them to start looking for other opportunities, laying them off, etc. These are all bullshit. You're firing someone. Luckily I'm not in HR, and this isn't HR advice.

I worked at a big company once. I was the designer in their pre-web marketing department. And to make a long story short, I was done. I'd been there for awhile, I wasn't crazy about recent changes in the company, I'd become kind of a prick to work with, and I was still young enough that I felt they owed me something. I should've left.

One day the president of the company comes into my office and tells me what a bad employee I'd become. (True.) He tells me I had two weeks to shape up or they'd fire me. I'd never been fired before! I hated the job, but I didn't want to be fired. I also needed the money. So I turned into a model employee for two weeks. (You can do anything for two weeks.) I mean, I did *everything* asked of me with a smile on my face. I honestly thought I'd averted being fired.

Two weeks later he comes into my office and tells me my attitude hasn't improved and fires me. I was devastated.

Hindsight is a wonderful thing. When I look back on that moment two things come to mind. First, I should have left that job a *lot* sooner. I was done. Second, I never had two weeks to shape up. The firing was done from the moment he gave me the warning. And I spent two weeks thinking I had two weeks to save my job. Which I didn't. (Actually, three things come to mind: I'd like to thank him for freeing up my time to learn web design.)

Because of this particular experience I decided that I would *never* let an employee think they had a chance they actually didn't. When one of my employees is on thin ice I let him know, and when I decide he's done, I let him know that.

I've had to fire a few people. I take no pleasure in it. But when someone's not doing the job, they're putting an undue burden on the other employees, especially at a small company. And it's not fair to them. It's also not fair to let someone continue in a job that you've decided they can't do.

Be clear in your communication with your employees. Give them regular updates on how they're doing. If they're not doing well, give them steps to correct the problem as well as a timeline for achieving those steps. Getting fired should never come as a surprise.

Being fired sucks. It sucks much more than firing someone. So be clear and be quick. And be humane, but make no mistake that it is their right to see you as the prick in that situation. And it is your responsibility to take the steps to make your company better.

Everyone I've ever fired has gone on to do well somewhere else.

CONCLUSION

I told you a lie at the beginning of this book. To be fair, I believed it when I said it. But I told you I was writing this book for you. I wasn't. I was writing it for me. Because this shit is hard.

Let's be honest. It's a pain in the ass to get up every morning and design stuff for people. Most of the time you're hitting your head against the wall, or going down the wrong path. Most of the work we do gets thrown out. Even the best of us have worse batting averages than ball players.

But those times when you get stuff right? Oh man, those are good times.

So I wrote this book to remind myself of those good times. To remind myself that the time I've spent beating my head against the wall, filling up a digital trash can with metaphorical crumpled up work, and being asked to make logos bigger, buttons brighter, and "jazzing things up" actually amounted to something. It amounted to something I could pass on to you. And it paid back all the designers who were kind enough to help *me* learn the craft.

There are no bad clients. Okay, maybe there are *some* bad clients. But they're not the problem. For too long now designers have complained that clients haven't behaved how they needed them to. You, my dears (and I love you all) have been the problem. You've ignored the parts of the job you either didn't like, felt uncomfortable doing, or didn't even know were your responsibility.

Maybe no one told you this was part of your job. Well, now I have.

We come from a strong line of kings and queens. People who have spent their lives making the world a better place than when they entered it. Some in small ways. Some in large ways.

Tibor Kalman. Victor Papanek. Paul Rand. Ray and Charles Eames. Dieter Rams. Erik Spiekermann. Zuzana Licko. Jeffrey Zeldman. Paula Scher. Thousands of people whose names are lost to history who signed the highways, the subways, our baseball cards, and our cities. And you. You are all designers. You are all as good or as weak as you choose to be. And you all have an opportunity to leave your mark of good work on the world. And I pray you use it well.

Now go do the thing.

RESOURCES

This is a list of items neither basic nor necessary. You don't need me to point those sorts of things out to you. Following are a few books and websites I hope will make you realize that you have a lot to learn, and get excited about that fact. Perpetual intellectual curiosity is the greatest resource a professional designer can have. Barring that, an island hideaway is nice.

Respect your elders

Design has been around longer than the internet has. Good designers have strong voices; listen to them.

- *Paul Rand: Conversations with Students,* Michael Kroeger
- *Design for the Real World,* Victor Papanek
- *Tibor Kalman, Perverse Optimist,* Peter Hall and Michael Bierut (Sadly out of print, you should get your hands on a copy. Maybe the library has it.)
- *Make it Bigger,* Paula Scher
- *Less and More: The Design Ethos of Dieter Rams,* Klaus Klemp and Keiko Ueki-Polet

Sell yourself

A career in design is one long pitch. Be prepared.

- *Life's a Pitch,* Roger Mavity and Stephen Bayley
- *P. T. Barnum: America's Greatest Showman,* Philip B. Kunhardt, Jr., et al.

Be grounded and well-rounded

Whatever type of design you do, your work exists in a space between physical artifacts and human attitudes and perceptions. Always keep this in mind.

- *Being Wrong,* Kathryn Schulz (Not only are you designing for fallible humans, you are one of them. Empathy and intellectual understanding will make you stronger and less of a jerk.)
- *The Language of Things,* Deyan Sudjic (It doesn't matter if you are an interactive designer, your work exists in context of the world. A marginally less angry companion to Papanek's book.)
- *The Information: A History, a Theory, a Flood,* James Gleick (If it's not stuff, it's information. We have too much of both.)
- *Managing Humans,* Michael Lopp (You'll probably have to work with some sort of humans in some sort of hierarchy; not only good for managers, but also the managed.)

Love what you do, and be very good at it

Read some autobiographies of people you admire and relate to for perspective. They don't have to be these. Life anecdotes are excellent fodder for design presentations, even if they aren't yours.

- *Life Itself: A Memoir,* Roger Ebert
- *Bossypants,* Tina Fey
- *Autobiography of Mark Twain,* Mark Twain
- *The Autobiography of Benjamin Franklin,* Benjamin Franklin

Internet weblogs

Smart people writing stuff.

- *Subtraction* by Khoi Vinh: http://subtraction.com
- *Ftrain* by Paul Ford: http://ftrain.com
- *You Are Not So Smart*: http://youarenotsosmart.com (More about how our brains fail us. Excellent anecdote to hubris.)

ACKNOWLEDGEMENTS

As difficult as it might be to write a book, I assure you that everyone within ten feet of me while I was writing suffered more than I did. My apologies across the board. You are all good people who deserved better than I was able to give you for the last few months.

This book wouldn't exist at all without Jeffrey Zeldman, who convinced me I needed to write it all down when I was afraid to; to Mandy Brown, who makes me sound so much smarter than I actually am; and to Jason Santa Maria, who makes it all look so good. I'm honored to be the brown stripe in A Book Apart's rainbow of awesomesauce.

My lawyer, Gabe Levine, who got the profanity clause removed from the book contract.

Katie Gillum, who workshopped a ton of this book with me on our podcast *Let's Make Mistakes* and helped me with outlines. Tina Lee, who read through too many rough drafts and was never afraid to tell me when something sucked. David McCreath who has been putting up with my rants for longer than anyone. And everyone at Mule who treats design as a job every day. To every past Mule employee who's had to deal with me learning how to do the job.

To everyone who gave me advice, feedback or stern talking to throughout the writing process. Michael Sippey, Andre Torrez, Amber Costley, Anil Dash, Alaina Browne, Mat Honan, Beth Callahan, Jeff Veen, Bryan Mason, Colleen Wainwright, Michele Catalano, Mike Essl, Mia Eaton, Josh and Kayla Cagan, Kristina Halvorson, Jen Bekman, Ryan Freitas, Ryan Carver, Rae Brune, Mike Kuniavsky, Elizabeth Goodman, Tina Roth Eisenberg, Amy Jane Gruber, and her husband, whose name escapes me.

To Erik Spiekermann, who disproves the axiom that meeting your idols will be a disappointment, and was kind enough to write the foreword to this book.

To every client—past, present, and future—who has entrusted me with their projects and made it possible for me to practice my craft and earn a living. Thank you.

A huge hug to my parents, Americo and Judite Monteiro, who were courageous enough to immigrate to a country where being a loud-mouthed jerk could be turned into an asset.

To my son Henry, who makes me want to be a better person, and whose respect means more to me than anything in the world. I owe you some Mario Kart games, kid. And to my baby momma, Tracey Long, who is helping me raise a wonderful boy.

A very special thank you to Annette Rankin, who has the hardest job in the world.

And, of, course, neither this book, nor our design studio, nor much of anything would be conceivable without Erika Hall, my partner in all things good and bad. Her inspiration, her prodding, her support, and her understanding make all things possible.

And thanks to everybody who skipped right to this page looking for your name. I hope you learned something either way.

INDEX

A

advertising 20-21

B

being nice 14
being wrong 73
blogging 21

C

cash flow 98-99
Caslon, William 9
client anxiety 60-61
client budgets 90-91
commencement fees 95-97
competing designers 85-86, 101-102, 105-106
comps from clients 84-86
conferences 21
content strategists 119-120
contract negotiations 50-52

D

Dash, Anil 32
deadlines 80-81
deposits. *See* commencement fees
developers 115-116
directing other designers 122-124

E

Eames, Ray and Charles 9, 130
elevator pitches 15
enforcing contracts 55
engineers 116-118
establishing a feedback cycle 76, 80-81
ethical responsibilities 28

F

feedback guidelines 78-79
firing people 127-129

G

Gillum, Katie 87
Gruber, John 121

H

Hall, Erika 2, 82, 110

I

indemnity 54
information designers 113-114
intellectual property transfers 53
internal dysfunctions 62-63
invoice approval 92-93

K

Kalman, Tibor 9, 130
Kickstart 33
kill fees. *See* termination fees

L

late payments 97-98
lawyers 47-50, 89, 98
leadership 124-129
Let's Make Mistakes 87
Levine, Gabe 48
Licko, Zuzana 9, 130
lines of credits 98
lowballing 43-44

M

maintaining relationships 16-17
marketers 118-119
market research 36
myth of the magical creative 6

N

negative feedback 71
networking 15-16

O

organizing client feedback 82-83
outbound client contacts 20

P

Papanek, Victor 9, 130
payment milestones. *See* structuring
   payments
payment terms 94-95
peer criticism 102-104
prescriptive feedback 79-80
presenting with a team 72-73
price negotiation 42-43
pricing 34-39
processes of design 58-61
professional development 121
project managers 111-112
proposals 40-41

R

Rams, Dieter 130
Rand, Paul 130
referrals 12-18
reluctant buyers 25
request for proposals 19
researchers 113

S

Scher, Paula 9, 130
screeners 18
secret to life 44
small jobs 38-39
Spiekermann, Erik 130
stakeholders 77
statements of work 52, 76
sticker shock 39-40
structuring payments 95-97
Super MoneyMaker 33

T

tailors 13, 31, 95
termination fees 53

U

understanding goals 7, 37, 57-58
user advocacy 9

W

waffling over decisions 63-64
warranties 54
wireframes 114-115
working for free 27
working with friends 56
working with other designers 107-110

Z

Zeldman, Jeffrey 9, 16, 130

ABOUT A BOOK APART

Web design is about multi-disciplinary mastery and laser focus, and that's the thinking behind our brief books for people who make websites. We cover the emerging and essential topics in web design and development with style, clarity, and, above all, brevity—because working designer-developers can't afford to waste time.

The goal of every title in our catalog is to shed clear light on a tricky subject, and do it fast, so you can get back to work. Thank you for supporting our mission to provide professionals with the tools they need to move the web forward.

COLOPHON

The text is set in FF Yoga and its companion, FF Yoga Sans, both by Xavier Dupré. Headlines and cover are set in Titling Gothic by David Berlow.

ABOUT THE AUTHOR

Mike Monteiro is the co-founder and design director of Mule Design, an interactive design studio founded in 2001 whose work has been called "delightfully hostile" by *The New Yorker*. He prefers elegant, simple sites with clear language that serve a real need. He prefers that designers have strong spines. All of his clients still talk to him.

Mike blogs frequently about the craft and business of design on muledesign.com, and can be heard weekly as the co-host of *Let's Make Mistakes* on muleradio.net. None of the terms Mike has coined are printable on a family website.

Originally, and emphatically, from Philadelphia, Mike now resides in San Francisco. When he's not at work he's out buying music on vinyl, reading comics, playing Mario Kart with his son Henry, and getting into arguments on Twitter. You can follow him as @Mike_FTW, but we're not liable for what you'll see.

He secretly really likes his dog.

Photo by Ryan Carver